MO1 40000 77066

SO-EIR-582

2-98

LOVE AS DEATH
IN *THE ICEMAN COMETH*
A Modern Treatment of an Ancient Theme
by *Winifred Dusenbury Frazer*

UNIVERSITY OF FLORIDA PRESS / GAINESVILLE, 1967

EDITORIAL COMMITTEE

Humanities Monographs

T. WALTER HERBERT, *Chairman*
Professor of English

G. PAUL MOORE
Professor of Speech

CHARLES W. MORRIS
Professor of Philosophy

REID POOLE
Professor of Music

C. A. ROBERTSON
Professor Emeritus of English

MELVIN E. VALK
Professor of German

AUBREY L. WILLIAMS
Professor of English

COPYRIGHT © 1967 BY THE BOARD OF
COMMISSIONERS OF STATE INSTITUTIONS
OF FLORIDA

LIBRARY OF CONGRESS
CATALOG CARD NO. 67-65495

PRINTED BY THE STORTER PRINTING COMPANY
GAINESVILLE, FLORIDA

CONTENTS

LOVE AS DEATH IN *THE ICEMAN COMETH*
A Modern Treatment of an Ancient Theme

INTRODUCTION

C entral to *The Iceman Cometh* in the language, in the setting, in the characters, and in the structure of the action, is the theme that love is death. From the title, with its implication that the bridegroom of love is the iceman of death, to the last shouted words of the chorus of men—about hot days under the willow trees, which are symbols of sex as well as of grief for death—the speeches are interspersed with metaphors and puns connoting that love and death are one. The setting is in a tomb-like back room and bar which the stage directions and remarks of the characters make obvious is a place of the dead rather than of the living. The characters themselves begin and end in a moribund state, from which they are at one point wooed almost to literal death. The action, as carried out in the four-act structure, although it cannot be said to be as explicit a representation of sexual intercourse ending in death as is Ionesco's *The Lesson*,[1] does nevertheless, by its repetitious pulsing in wave-like rhythm and its tension in the buildup of scenes, convey the pattern of the earthy iceman joke which O'Neill said he had in mind while writing the play.

The relationship of love to death, in the metaphor of Cupid's arrow as a deadly weapon, goes far back in mythology and deep in man's psyche. English poetry abounds in complaints upon Cupid's fatal dart, which pierces the fleshly breast with bleeding wound. Michael Drayton, for example, in "Cupid, I Hate Thee,"[2] pleads with the little archer to forbear the use of his weapon and to take up the harp, so that he may play for Venus "whilst with Mars she holdeth her old way." Love and death, of course, are also related in the metaphoric, sexual use of "to die." And following Freud's description of the "primal instincts of Eros and death,"[3] their relationship has been discussed by numerous critics. Denis de Rougemont explains "the kinship of the fighting and the pro-

1. Bernard F. Dukore, "The Theatre of Ionesco: A Union of Form and Substance," *Educational Theatre Journal*, XIII (1961), 174-81.
2. *Six Centuries of Great Poetry*, ed. Robert Penn Warren and Albert Erskine (New York, 1960), p. 119.
3. *Civilization and Its Discontents*, trans. James Strachey (New York, 1962), pp. 64-69.

1

creative instincts," and the "warlike language of love" in chivalric literature: "A lover *besieged* his lady. He delivered *amorous assaults* on her virtue. He *pressed her closely.* He *pursued* her. He sought to *overcome* the final *defences* of her modesty, and *to take them by surprise.*"[4] His thesis is that our acceptance of the symbols of courtly mysticism leads us "from desire to death via *passion*," for passion means suffering, which if we consider it fruitful, leads us to embrace killing.

Even the modern psychoanalyst Erich Fromm, who questions Freud's contention that "the striving toward death and toward life are two biologically given tendencies," does believe that necrophilia exists as man's "most malignant pathology." He claims: "So many people are in love with death," that they "want war."[5] Leslie Fiedler, in *Love and Death in the American Novel*,[6] sees the perversion of love in America as resulting in a lack of masculinity in the male and a consequent wish for death. Christopher Hollis, in "The Love of Death," claims that "the real cause of war is the love of death," and warns that we must beware of the "secret place in our soul which wants destruction for its own sake."[7] Young Dag Hammarskjöld reveals the erotic appeal of death in a passage in his diary: "Tomorrow we shall meet,/ Death and I—/ And he shall thrust his sword/ Into one who is wide awake."[8]

Man as the bridegroom is lost—in all kinds of poetry from the most sublime to the nursery rhyme, the connection between love and death is clear. "The Happy Courtship and Merry Marriage of Cock Robin and Jenny Wren" is followed in an old nursery rhyme book by, alas, "The Doleful Death of the Bridegroom," or "Who Killed Cock Robin?"[9] It was the sparrow with Cupid's bow and arrow naturally who "killed" the "cock." Spenser complains frequently of Cupid's weapon: "how great the smart/ Of those whom thou dost wound:/ Full many hast thou pricked to

4. *Love in the Western World* (New York, 1956), pp. 244-45.
5. "Creators and Destroyers," *Saturday Review*, XLVII, 1 (Jan. 4, 1964), 24.
6. New York, 1960.
7. *Horizon*, XVIII, 105 (Sept., 1948), 156-69.
8. Max Ascoli, "On Reading Hammarskjöld," *The Reporter* (May 20, 1965), pp. 37-40.
9. *The Oxford Dictionary of Nursery Rhymes*, ed. Iona and Peter Opie (Oxford: Clarendon Press, 1951), p. 129.

the hart. . . ."[10] In the spiritual life of man, as the parable which O'Neill used for the title shows, love and death seem inextricably combined. Erotic effusions of the saints concerning their eternal union with God are common. In Nikos Kazantzakis' *The Fratricides*, Father Yanaros, badly burned in a church fire, exclaims: "I felt that the fire which had burned me, which had engulfed me, was You—You, my Lord! 'This is what love means,' I cried, 'this is the way man merges with woman and God with the soul of man.'" And the old priest goes to lie with his Lord "upon the Bier among the wildflowers."[11]

O'Neill may see Eros and Thanatos as the two faces of man; he may see Venus and Mars as lovers; he may see a perversion of love in America which leads to a preference for death; he may see Christian love of death as prelude to eternal life; but beyond all, or perhaps in combination with all, he sees the grotesque ambiguity in the fact that love, which says "Let us be true to one another," and which alone perhaps can save mankind from death, actually results in man's destruction. Only through a dirty joke can he face the supreme absurdity that the longed-for bridegroom of love is really the iceman of death. With sardonic humor he transforms Jesus, the spiritual bridegroom (although in the metaphor in Matthew connotations of erotic love are not missing, for Matthew was no Paul), into the sensuous iceman. He had in mind, he says, the dirty joke in which the husband, calling upstairs to his wife—"Has the iceman come yet?"—gets the reply, "Not yet, but he's breathin' hard."[12] To O'Neill the bridegroom who "comes" signifies the benumbed state of man's body and spirit, as he is faced with the truth that love is only an illusion—nothing better than an iceman-and-the-wife joke popular in an era when the iceman walked freely in upon the negligee-clad wife. Musing on this kind of vulgar joke, O'Neill must have felt grim vindication of his thesis that man lives by illusion, as he read uncomplimentary first-night reviews of *The Iceman* and recognized how little the critics penetrated the despair evoked in him by what he saw as the truth that, to man, love is death.

10. "Amoretti," *The Complete Poetical Works of Spenser*, ed. R. E. Neil Dodge (Cambridge, Mass., 1936), p. 735.
11. New York, 1964, pp. 146-47.
12. Arthur and Barbara Gelb, *O'Neill: A Biography* (New York, 1962), p. 831.

3

A detailed examination of the play through its setting, its characters, and the structure of its action illustrates how O'Neill makes this truth explicit. The play, which covers parts of a two-day, two-night period in a dark back room and bar of a rundown West Side tenement hotel, concerns the attempt of the formerly ebullient hardware salesman, Hickey, to make each of a dozen drunken dreamers face the truth about himself. From this action emerges the major theme of the play that belief in love is the greatest of man's illusions.

1. SETTING

The setting, which in four acts includes views of Harry Hope's back room, of the bar itself, and of the barroom, appropriately emphasizes the funereal nature of the existence lived by the drunks within its walls. In Thornton Wilder's *Our Town*, the deceased in the cemetery are very much alive, but in O'Neill's play the survivors in the Hell Hole are essentially dead, as the metaphors they use and the stage directions testify. The name of the proprietor might seem to be an exception, were it not that his initials are the same as those for his establishment. But in spite of suffering all the ills of Pandora's box, these moldering wrecks feel that Harry Hope lives up to his name by providing the refuge without which all would perish. In this Bottom of the Sea Rathskeller, his bar is the shoal which the men crossed when they put out to sea, but even as Bedrock Bar it also dispenses Hope, delusive Hope, which always says, "Tomorrow all will be well," and which has the crow as its emblem because its cry *cras, cras* in Latin means tomorrow.

At this "last resort" establishment, the back room is separated from the bar by a "dirty black curtain"; two windows "so glazed with grime one cannot see through them" look out on a backyard; the walls are "splotched, peeled, stained, and dusty"; two wall bracket lights on the left and two at the back provide the only light. In this tomb-like place sit Larry, scratching himself because of lice, and nine other bedraggled specimens of male humanity in various stages of deterioration. Carrying out sea analogies, Larry says of the others, "Their ships are long since looted and scuttled and sunk on the bottom," and agrees with Rocky that "Willie sure is on de bottom" and that "General" Wetjoen's authority is like a "memory of the drowned." Larry says of himself, "I'm drowned and contented on the bottom of a bottle." Rosamond Gilder's epithet for the scene—"the very home of oblivion, a Sargasso Sea of human flotsam"—is very apt.[1] When Hickey arrives later and exhorts the dreamers, "Let yourself sink down to the bottom of the sea. Rest in Peace," he reveals his lack of per-

1. Oscar Cargill, *Intellectual America: Ideas on the March* (New York, 1941), p. 207.

ception that the bottom is where they now lie, and that *Requiescat in pace* could well be the inscription above Hope's bar.

Hope's back room as an earthly house of death is an even more frequent object of metaphoric jibes. "Dis dump is like de morgue wid all dese bums passed out," according to Rocky. To Larry it's the No Chance Saloon, the End of the Line Cafe, which the cops consider as "harmless as a graveyard." The place is a tomb for Harry Hope, who has never set foot out of it in twenty years. And Jimmy is assured that he is East of Suez, where "East is West, and tomorrow is yesterday," while it sometimes gives Hope "the graveyard fantods." After dawn arrives and the dim wall bracket lights are turned off, the room becomes "drabber and dingier than ever," visibly denying the proverb that it's always darkest *before* the dawn. Margie, coming in from a night's work, remarks aptly, "Jees, Poil, it's de Morgue wid all de stiffs on deck." Chiding Larry for not having died yet, she gets the reply, "But I'm waiting impatiently for the end." Cora's comment is the same— "Jees, de Morgue on a rainy Sunday night!"—as is her question to Larry: "Ain't you croaked yet?" He follows suit with, "It's damned tiring, this waiting for the end."

Even Hickey, who should be the life bringer, finds that his friends react to his proposed celebration as if it were a funeral. To Larry's accusation that the salesman's peace may be poison, Hope responds, "Bejees, Larry, you're always croaking about something to do with death," as indeed he is, but as the situation seems in this case to warrant; for Hickey sinks down "in complete exhaustion" while the men stare and Hope exclaims: "Stone cold sober and dead to the world!" That same death which has hung heavy over the setting and characters throughout the long act comes in for ridicule when Mosher enlivens the crowd with a tale about a charlatan, old Doc, who died because he didn't follow his own advice to drink a pint of whiskey before breakfast each day and stay away from work. He died without achieving his aim of filling every "vacant cemetery lot left in this glorious country." But Mosher surmises, to the delight of his audience, that old Doc is probably making "suckers of the damned" right now by selling them "snake oil for a bad burn." The damned in the hell-hole of Hope's back room might well be laughing at themselves. The echoing roar of merriment—hollow as it may seem—is, however, less sinister than Hickey's drowsy muttering from the

6

dead world of his perturbed mind, which at the end of Act I puzzles the staring, resentful drunks.

In Act II the walls of the back room have been slightly cleaned but now have a "splotchy, leprous look," which the red ribbons on the light brackets intensify. The circular tables have been pushed together to make a long, improvised banquet table, on which are set bottles of bar whiskey within easy reach of each guest. Several wrapped birthday presents and a cake for Hope's midnight birthday party complete the depressing scene. Without success, the girls—Cora, Pearl, and Margie—try to give the place a festive air. They have borrowed tablecloths from a neighboring beanery and are arranging some flowers in a large schooner glass from the bar. They admire the basket full of quarts of champagne which Hickey brings. And Cora, at the height of the celebration, pathetically bangs out a tune on the piano. But the misery which Hickey has instilled in all of them as they face the morrow casts a pall which none of the preparations can allay. "An undercurrent of nervous irritation" causes bitter words and inimical responses among them all. Hope's angry order to Cora, "Hey, you dumb tart, quit banging that box," is especially shattering to a happy atmosphere because the kindly old honoree of the evening is usually genial.

Charges between Hickey and Larry, who continues to deride Hickey's aim of making the men face reality, set the tone for the act. When Hickey arrives with the presents, he designates Larry "Old Cemetery, the Barker for the Big Sleep," an epithet which Rocky and the girls gleefully pick up and use later. To Larry's speculation that Hickey has brought the cold touch of death with him, Rocky replies, "You got croakin' on the brain, Old Cemetery." And when Larry later derides all the festive preparations as "a second feast of Belshazzar, with Hickey to do the writing on the wall!" Cora cries, "Aw, shut up, Old Cemetery." Larry's designation is very appropriate, for in spite of Rocky's trying to cheer up the crowd with, "What is dis, a funeral?" and Hickey's protesting into the "dead silence," "We don't want corpses at this feast," the doom of death hangs over the celebration, as over Belshazzar's.

Hickey seems to the men to be something of a devil in the way he manipulates them and in the pact they have inadvertently made with him. Hickey's claim, "I can size up guys, and turn 'em inside out, better than I ever could," is obviously true, but what they doubt is his insistence that the process of facing reality

7

will bring contentment. Also they fear him and feel, like Parritt, that "there's something not human behind his damned grinning and kidding." It is the devil's method to appear charming and to supply life's champagne while he gets a grasp upon the unfortunate soul who succumbs. The Hell Hole in Act II undergoes some physical transformation, but with Hickey presiding, the tension and suffering of the victims progressively increase. Hickey, who pretends to play the part of a guiding Virgil, is really wooing the men to permanent damnation.

Act III moves from the back room to the barroom itself with the bar at rear and swinging doors to the street on stage right. Over the mirror behind the bar are framed photographs of Tammany politicians Richard Croker and Big Tim Sullivan. The fact that politicians rather than the usual painting of Custer's Last Stand or Aphrodite on a bed of flowers hold the place of honor means that Hope's dreams lie in the realm of the political rather than in the heroic or amorous. Flanking the Tammany Hall big shots are framed lithographs of John L. Sullivan and Gentleman Jim Corbett in ring costume, these latter reflecting the determined masculine atmosphere which prevails in Hope's bar. The only act which takes place in the cold light of day, the scene is nevertheless dark, because although it is a hot summer morning outside, the sun does not hit the windows. The iceman presides at Hope's bar, as the mood of the night before is intensified. Rocky's comment on the party, "Jees, what a funeral," could well be said of the *today* which is no longer *tomorrow*. Hickey has brought the "touch of death" with him, as Larry reaffirms, when Joe charges at Chuck with a bread knife, Chuck starts to defend himself with a whiskey bottle, and Rocky backs him up with a short-barreled revolver. Harry Hope and Jimmy Tomorrow "look like dey was goin' to de electric chair," as Hickey urges them to leave the tomb, or perhaps it is the womb, which the bar seems to them. There is a bluff in their manner suggesting "the last march of the condemned." When Harry returns, he slumps into a chair, feeling all in, "Like a corpse, bejees." Hugo assures Hope that he does indeed "look dead," but for whatever comfort it is worth, adds, "I feel I am dying too." Rocky verifies that Hope "does look like he'd croaked." And Larry chimes in once more against Hickey: "It's the peace of death you've brought him." The gift—a watch engraved with name and date—which Hickey has pre-

8

sented to Hope has perhaps impressed upon the easy-going old proprietor that the time is now.

Sordid as the Hell Hole may be, it is not so terrifying as the bright street outside. The pain of living is at least dulled here. Being pushed out through the swinging doors into a harsh world of reality is an undesired birth, and in the next act all retreat again to the womb where they float uncomprehending in the amniotic fluid of alcohol.[2] Larry in the beginning quotes Heine as saying that death is good but "the best of all were never to be born." The men therefore try to avoid emerging, but with Hickey applying the forceps, they are propelled forth one by one—still-born, however, under Hickey's inexpert obstetrics. The lack of any feeling of the generative force of woman in the play adds to the theme of the mortality of loving. It is not surprising that in the next act all the men return, unregenerated and almost dead. One is reminded that in Sartre's *No Exit,* even when the three characters are given the choice of emerging, they cannot bring themselves to depart from hell.

More death-like than the first three, Act IV opens on the back room and bar in the very early morning of the second day after Hickey's arrival. An air of "oppressive stagnation" prevails in which the characters all sit in a "numb stupor" like "wax figures" and have a "quality of insensibility." In the "sodden silence" Hickey accuses the men of "acting like a lot of stiffs cheating the under-taker." Jimmy's face wears a "wax-figure blankness that makes it look embalmed." The condition of the characters, suitable for the hell-hole setting, makes an appropriate climax to a play in which they have spoken throughout in necrophilic metaphors. There is considerable affection for death in the tone which Cora and Rocky use in addressing Larry as Old Cemetery; in which Margie and Cora note, "It's de Morgue wid all de stiffs on deck"; in which Hickey advises, "Let yourself sink down to the bottom of the sea"; in which Rocky remarks of the birthday party, "Jees, what a funeral!"; in which Larry insists that Hickey has brought "the touch of death" with him; in which he later intones, "May the Chair bring him peace at last"; and in which he gruesomely con-

2. According to Julian N. Hartt, *The Lost Image of Man* (Baton Rouge, La., 1963), pp. 121-22, "In the Freudian account the craving for death is a project for peace: it is the peace of the womb-life rather than the peace of absolute nullity."

cludes, "All things . . . grin at me from the one skull of death." The huge cynical joke which the drunks in this worldly Hades find amusing lacks Frost's light tone—"Forgive, oh Lord, my little jokes on thee/ And I'll forgive thy great big one on me." The joke, though smutty, is "dead-serious," as the sepulchral setting in a charnel house, the ossified condition of the victims, and their funereal metaphors make evident.

In *Hughie,* written a year after *The Iceman* and set in a dingy hotel lobby at four o'clock in the morning, outside sounds penetrate the consciousness of the night clerk. Elevated trains clatter by, trash cans are battered about on the sidewalk, and the sirens of fire engines bring the outside world in. It is true that *Hughie* is a kind of "Iceman's ice cube," but Erie, although "he will always be in death," nevertheless is "in the midst of life,"[3] which is not true of the characters of *The Iceman.* Like a crypt encased in layers of concrete, Hope's bar excludes the outside world, eliminates the difference between day and night, and underlines the cadaverous nature of its denizens.

In spite of the fact that Harry Hope presides, there might be placed above the entrance to this hell the motto, Abandon Hope; for even the life of which these lost characters dream is mercilessly disparaged. The cynicism expressed by the characters in metaphors of death in a morgue-like setting is so overpowering that the satire of contemporary social ills goes almost unnoticed; but this satire creates derision for the social, political, religious, economic, ethical, and educational life of the twentieth century and hence implements the dominant theme of the desirability of death by pointing up the undesirability of all of life, as part of the background against which the players act their parts.

Foremost is satire of the Anarchist movement, of which Larry, Parritt, Parritt's mother, and Hugo have all been a part. "To hell with the Movement" is Larry's present attitude toward it, and Parritt has always been disillusioned with syndicalism because his mother and her friends neglected him for it. She has always acted the free woman, but enslaved him to the Movement, and condemned him for not having the life-consuming interest in it that she has. Apparently she has engendered hatred in Larry as well as in her son through devotion to this cause, which Parritt now calls "a damned foreign pipe dream." Only a fool, O'Neill is

3. *Time,* Jan. 1, 1965.

saying along with Parritt, could believe that a gang is going "to change the world by shooting off their loud traps on soapboxes and sneaking around blowing up a lousy building or bridge." Forgetting human love for a socialistic cause has led to tragedy for Parritt and his mother, and Hope denounces Larry as "a damned old fool Anarchist I-Won't-Worker," obviously in derogation of the IWW. With like sharp wit, he exclaims that "a Harry Hope revolution" and a "dispossess bomb" on their tails may blow Larry and Hugo out of the hell-hole and make their Movement move.

It is through the character of Hugo that the bitterest truth about the Movement is exposed. Full of the jargon of socialism, he reveals, when drunk, that he is not in sympathy with the common man, but only with getting on top himself. He is a "type Anarchist," an "alien radical" mouthing the epithets of his kind—Capitalist swine! Bourgeois stool pigeons!—who then reveals his snobbery by calling Rocky "damned bourgeois Wop," by insisting like a second Robespierre that he will hang Hickey when the great Day comes, "the first one of all on de first lamppost," and by proclaiming maliciously that soon the "leedle proletarians" will feed on hot dogs like "beautiful leedle hogs" beneath the willow trees. Like Parritt's mother, who "doesn't want anyone to be free but herself," Hugo, who has formerly spent ten years in solitary for the cause, reveals that he now abhors those whom he pretends to wish to free. Pulling all the stops, O'Neill lampoons the Socialist-Anarchist movement with an outworn minstrel-show joke, in which Joe defines an Anarchist as a man who blows his money in on bombs and a Socialist as a man who shares his wealth, but who, if broke, is a "no-good bastard" as well. Larry sees all the "practical wisdom of the world in that little parable." Then, bringing satire of the Movement to bear on the main theme of the play, Larry reminds Hugo, "It's not Bakunin's ghost you ought to pray to in your dreams, but to the great Nihilist, Hickey! He's started a movement that'll blow up the world!"

A second object of O'Neill's contempt is military heroism as shown in "Captain" Lewis and "General" Wetjoen. Cecil Lewis goes shirtless in order to display the scar he got from a native spear in the Boer War, and both dream of "the brave days in South Africa when they tried to murder each other." Most ludicrous is that they came to America to work in the Boer War spectacle at the St. Louis Fair and have since sat dreaming about their great exploits. Wetjoen says that it's a great shame that he missed Lewis at the battle of Moder River, and Cecil counters by claiming the British should have nabbed Wetjoen and put him in a cage of baboons. When drunk they relive the war so actually that Wetjoen mistakes Joe for a black Kaffir. Under Hickey's sobering influence, the truth emerges that Cecil stole regimental money for gambling and that Wetjoen connived a surrender in order to make his personal escape. So it is not a case of heroes gone bad, but of dastards pretending to be heroes. The war hero, O'Neill makes out, is nothing but a cheap actor in a spectacle at a world's fair on the stage of life.

A third realm which comes in for disparagement is the political. Harry Hope, in spite of being out of Tammany politics for twenty years, still has enough friends to protect him from the law. His place is never raided and he keeps recalling the race for alderman, which "was all fixed." Pat McGloin has been a police lieutenant, thrown off the force when his graft became too obvious. "An old grafting flatfoot," Hope calls him and quotes Bessie as saying, "I hope they send him to Sing Sing for life." McGloin wants to get back on the police force, where "there's fine pickings these days." Willie Oban, with drunken verve, offers to take McGloin's case for reinstatement, although he considers him "guilty as hell," and if Willie cannot get the case legally reopened, he has found information that he can use for blackmail. Since his father had been active in the criminal world, he knows a thing or two about how to pervert the law through graft and blackmail. Mosher, as an old circus conman, good enough to have "short-changed the Keeper of the Mint," has managed to evade the law. Joe gives the lowdown on political corruption in his account of his gambling joint: "I run wide open for years and pays my sugar on de dot, and de cops and I is friends." Of course the three prostitutes depend on Rocky and Chuck to keep them clear of the law by bribing the cops. The whole political and associated legal scene, according to O'Neill, is one for scorn.

Satire on social status emerges in characters as diverse as Willie Oban and the prostitutes. Willie has been badly hurt at Harvard by the snobbery which made him socially unacceptable. A brilliant student, he says, "I was accepted socially with all the warm cordiality that Henry Wadsworth Longfellow would have shown a

12

drunken Negress dancing the cancan at high noon on Brattle Street." Nevertheless Willie claims to add an air of culture to Hope's bar and even an intellectual royalty, indicating a certain snobbery on his part, too. But utterly debased, he puts on rags and resorts to beggary in *Three-Penny-Opera* style. The three prostitutes, on the other hand, while making no claim to royalty, are very sensitive about being called whores, though they admit to being tarts with no revulsion. The elegant hostess, worrying about protocol at an important dinner, could not be more particular, and semantics make as important a difference to Chuck and Rocky, who in the one case are pimps, but in the other bartenders who fend for the girls out of kindness and take care of their money. Chuck and Cora even plan to attain the status of marriage. Shaw's Doolittle regrets having to take this step into bourgeois morality, but Chuck and Cora look forward to the day when their relationship will be acceptable in the eyes of society. Joe's status as a "white" Negro is pretty well assured when all are drunk, but when sober, Margie says, "Just because we act nice to him, he gets a swelled nut! If dat ain't a coon all over!" and Lewis feels so low himself he is honored that a Negro "would lower himself to sit beside me." The niceties of social rank are also neatly satirized in Hugo's meticulous threadbare clothing and flowing Windsor tie of the foreign intellectual and in the designations of Captain and General for Lewis and Wetjoen, as well as in the tomorrow dreams, all of which involve some restoration of social status.

Religion comes in for derision mainly through Hickey, who, according to his own story, fulfilled the old saying: "Ministers' sons are sons of guns." He says that it only handed him a laugh to hear his old man "whooping up hell fire and scaring those Hoosier suckers into shelling out their dough." Of course Hickey admits that he learned selling from his preacher father, and we hear echoes of revivalism in his claim: "Brothers and Sisters. This peace is real! It's a fact! I know! Because I've got it! Here! Now! Right in front of you!" Larry, recognizing the style, taunts Hickey about his "sawdust trail to salvation" and his conversion to "this great peace." Hickey is proud of the fact that he "didn't fall for the religious bunk," but he is not above using his father's methods. As a hardware salesman (hardware being a slang term for counterfeit money) he uses the same "knack of sales gab" and "line of bull" by which he tries to sell the hoped-for converts a specious peace.

Mosher takes a crack at Hickey's revivalistic methods when he tells Larry, "Glad to see Brother Hickey hasn't corrupted you to temperance." And Hope compares him at the end to "a bughouse preacher escaped from an asylum." The big Reform which Hickey preaches is natural, he says, because "My old man used to whale salvation into my heinie with a birch rod." But admiration for the father "who could sell those Hoosier hayseeds building lots along the Golden Street" makes Hickey continue in the selling line, whether it be of pans or peace.

Besides Hickey, who exemplifies satirically the revivalist preacher, Willie Oban furnishes several contemptuous remarks about the ministry. He asserts that, according to legend, Waldo Emerson composed the dirty rap-rap-rap ballad while trying to write a sermon, but it is his own belief that Jonathan Edwards wrote both words and music. In the light of O'Neill's distaste for the white New England meeting house which warped the Mannons, it is not hard to believe that it is he speaking through Willie. Later this brilliant but degenerate young drunk claims that the ballad, which he learned at Harvard, "was composed in a wanton moment by the Dean of the Divinity School . . . while sobering up in a Turkish bath." Whether religion is on a hayseed or an ivy-league level, the playwright has only scorn for it.

And O'Neill, like Mark Twain, also has no use for false sentimentality. Throughout the play are speeches paraphrasing, with satirical intent, commonplace phrases from poetry and melodrama: Jimmy Tomorrow's "Marjorie's favorite song was Loch Lomond. . . . You were lucky, Harry. Bessie died. But there are more bitter sorrows than losing the woman one loves by the hand of death"; Lewis' "England in April. . . . The old veldt has its points, I'll admit, but it isn't home—especially home in April"; Jimmy's "Boer and Briton, each fought fairly and played the game till the better man won and then we shook hands. We are all brothers within the Empire united beneath the flag on which the sun never sets"; Willie's "'Dear college days, with pleasure rife! The grandest gladdest days of life!'"; Cora's "He says Joisey's de best place [for a farm] and I says Long Island because we'll be near Coney"; Mosher's about the circus, "The greatest life on earth with the greatest show on earth! The grandest crowd of regular guys ever gathered under one tent!"; Hope's "Poor old Bessie! . . . A sweeter

14

woman never drew breath"; Parritt's "I'm from old American pio-
neer stock"; and Hugo's repeated "The days grow hot, O Babylon!
'Tis cool beneath thy willow trees!" False emotion under a veneer
of rhetoric was anathema to O'Neill.

Having in the first ten minutes of the play derided faith, religion, truth, philosophy, wisdom, and the beauty of human nature, O'Neill then continues in specific terms to derogate social
movements, military heroism, American politics, social pretension,
revivalism, and sentimentalized rhetoric. Doris Alexander says of
O'Neill as a social critic: "His criticism of the state extended to
the people in the state, and when he rejected hope for the state,
he rejected hope for humanity, and thus was left with a total
negativism, so that nothing was left for him but annihilation,
death."[4] Larry, in refusing to hear Parritt's confession, claims,
"Honor or dishonor, faith or treachery are nothing to me but the
opposites of the same stupidity which is ruler and king of life,
and in the end they rot into dust in the same grave." Life is
merely "The Feast of All Fools, with brass bands playing!" According to "De old Foolosopher," "the truth has no bearing on
anything," and to die is a better choice than to join in the false
celebration of living.

In the afterworld of Hope's bar the characters sit like semi-
corporeal ghosts, haunted by dreams of another life. Here the
body functions as a seemingly bottomless tankard down which the
rotgut pours. Love is absent from the scenes portrayed in Hope's
establishment, for the mercenary sale of this commodity by the
prostitutes necessarily takes place offstage; and the unanimously
destructive affairs in the past lives of the characters are shadowy
memories, or, in Hickey's case, the subject of a lengthy rational-
ization of his love-murder of Evelyn. Hickey, contending that
"it's all there, at the start, everything that happened afterwards,"
emphasizes the inevitability of love's resulting in death.

And so, with this as the play's thesis, O'Neill provides the bleak
setting which underlines man's doom. Jesus, in speaking of love
in the afterlife, makes a strange parallel between love and the
double meaning of death which fascinates O'Neill. When the
Sadducees question Jesus about the wife who had more than one
husband—In the resurrection whose wife will the woman be?—

4. "O'Neill as Social Critic," *American Quarterly*, VI (Winter, 1954),
349-63.

he replies that the resurrected "neither marry nor are given in marriage, for they cannot die any more." Father Marc Oraison points out that this text from Luke illustrates a "strange notation of a bond between genital sexuality and death."[5] Of course the passage can be said to mean that in Heaven procreation is not necessary since no one dies; but it also implies perhaps that without a body sexual climax is impossible.[6]

In the hell-hole the corpse-like individuals are bereft of the ability to love and are as in death. Since they are not the resurrected but the condemned, the aura of the scene is one of nihilism. The hope which might seem personified in the name of the proprietor is belied in his description as a "bag of bones," and the others of life's victims become "sunk in a numb stupor which is impervious to stimulation." The four dark scenes, punctuated by the black curtain which separates the bar from the back room, supply the appropriate setting for a drama on which love casts a death-like pall, as the bridegroom proves to be the iceman.

5. *Le mystère humain de la sexualité* (Paris, 1966), excerpts (trans. Leslie Timan) in *Ramparts,* V, 7 (Jan., 1967), 42-43.

6. In a later century Shakespeare, with the same kind of *double-entendre* which fascinates O'Neill, has the distraught Lear cry out: "I will die bravely, like a smug bridegroom" (*King Lear,* IV.vi). And certainly St. Paul's suggestion that it is better to marry than to burn implies that the purpose of marriage is sexual, as does the passage from Luke.

2. CHARACTERS

As to his characters, O'Neill, having lived as an alcoholic in the early Hell-Hole days, did not need to read a book to know that alcoholism is a form of suicide, nor that although it is in one sense an attempt to escape from the forces making for quick death by gun or poison, it is in the long run a method of self-destruction, and an even more painful one because of its prolongation of the act of dying. O'Neill's bums all seek the oblivion of death, and yet painfully stave it off by living on dreams and drink. Some critics see optimism in the friendly comradeship and ebullience re-established when it seems that Hickey, the do-gooder, or the psychiatrist in socio-medical terms, or the missionary-savior in religious terms, is, by his own admission, crazy. But these critics minimize the truth that although the road to death through drink is slightly longer, it is no less desperate than the shorter way. In fact, if Larry be taken as the voice of O'Neill, he most approves of Parritt's quick death.

O'Neill also understands the alcoholic's ambivalent attitudes of love and hate. The infantile revenge reaction of the alcoholic against hated love-objects whom he yet fears to lose, is clear in many of the characters, who reveal inadvertently their hatred for those they claim to adore. Harry Hope muses mournfully about his wife, dead for twenty years, of whom the memory is so keen that he sometimes can "see her in every room just as she used to be." He further recalls that when she died he "didn't have the heart" for anything and so gave up the race for alderman, and with even more woe he claims, "I've never set foot out of this house since the day I buried her." But later when Hickey has made him face reality, Hope blurts out, "Bejees, you're a worse gabber than that nagging bitch, Bessie, was." And much to the amazement of Rocky, who is perhaps the only one sober enough to be aware of the incongruity of Hope's swearing at his adored wife (except for Larry, who knew it all the time), the bereaved husband lets slip another such epithet, "that nagging old hag, Bessie." It appears that Bessie's having "made" him make friends with everyone, for which Hope has given her so much praise, was really part of the nagging he resented. From the Freudian view,

17

Hope appears in the role of son to a demanding mother, full of guilt feelings for having replaced his father, and resenting his mother's control while paradoxically experiencing a childish dependency and fear of losing her favor. Pretending love, he yet rejoiced when her death removed the goading which had kept him in political life.

Hickey goes further than enjoying his wife's death. He kills her with the very gun which he had given her for protection. After relating at length how intensely he had always loved her, he explains that he killed her in order to ease her suffering from his drunken binges. But his words—"Well, you know what you can do with your pipe dreams now, you damned bitch"—expose his true state of mind. He is horrified at his own revelation—more horrified than Hope had been because he is sober. "I couldn't have said that," he cries, "I loved Evelyn better than anything in life."

It is a strange relationship that makes death of the beloved more desirable than erotic love but that seems connected with erotic love. Both men had had (or wished it to be thought that they had had) an ardent sexual relationship; yet when death as the bridegroom took their wives, they were not jealous but pleased. Perhaps the fact that they refer to their wives as bitches also implies a kind of heated love which to them was smothering. Only through the death of these women could they gain a feeling of virility. Hickey is astonished to remember, when he starts to display Evelyn's picture, that he has torn it up. He has symbolically destroyed the very image of her whom he claims to have adored. His last, and perhaps most, erotic action toward her was killing her in bed. Hemingway's dying hero in *The Snows of Kilimanjaro* says to his wife: "I'd like to destroy you a few times in bed." "Yes. That's the good destruction. That's the way we're made to be destroyed," she replies. Hickey explains: "It would have been easy to find a way out if she hadn't loved me so much. Or if I hadn't loved her. But as it was, there was only one possible way. I had to kill her."

This is a virulent *Liebestod*, even though Hickey will die somewhat later than Evelyn. The perfect romantic love, achievable only in death, O'Neill shows us, is only the bitterest hatred. Hope's overpowering love for his dead Bessie has existed only since her death, for as Hickey tells him, "She was always on your neck,

18

making you have ambition and go out and do things, when all you wanted was to get drunk in peace." And all Hickey's jokes about his wife and the iceman really expressed his desire for her to belong to the iceman. He had so far convinced his friends of Hope's bar that there might have been something between Evelyn and the iceman that Hope exclaims, "Somebody croaked your Evelyn, eh? Bejees, my bets are on the iceman!" And later, when it appears that Hickey has shot Evelyn himself, Chuck sympathizes, "Yuh mean she really was cheatin' on him? Den I don't blame de guy—" The irony in these wrong surmises is evident later when Hickey proclaims that he killed her himself—but for love, not revenge.

In Parritt's case it is his mother, rather than a wife, whose destruction he has wrought, but his case is not very different from Hope's or Hickey's—he professes to have loved her, but wants her dead. He has killed her, not bodily, but effectively, by betraying the cause for which she lived—a kind of double death for her. Parritt reveals the truth by degrees, for the guilt which overcomes him makes him continually protest too much, as it does Hope and Hickey, of the depth of his love. Even after he has admitted his betrayal, he insists, "I still love her." And near the end of the play in response to Hickey's, "I loved Evelyn. Even as a kid," Parritt echoes, "I loved Mother, Larry." But his complaints—that she was "too busy with the Movement," had nothing "soft or sentimental" about her, objected to his "going around with tarts" though his own home was like "living in a whorehouse" —increase in intensity as he confesses to the one person in the world who can absolve him of guilt. His motive for betraying the Movement he changes from "duty to country" to "just for money" but claims until nearly the end of the play that he thought his mother would be safe.

Continuously, however, his thoughts of his mother seem inextricably involved with those of Hickey and Evelyn. In trying to express his fear of Hickey, Parritt muses: "It's that queer feeling he gives me that I'm mixed up with him some way. I don't know why, but it started me thinking about Mother—as if she was dead." He absent-mindedly responds several times to comments about Evelyn as if they were about his mother. Hickey has felt that he and Parritt are "members of the same lodge," and that Parritt is having trouble with himself, and although Parritt has

19

tried to deny ties of guilt, he cannot repress his subconscious reactions. Thus when Rocky mentions the possibility of Evelyn's having committed suicide, Parritt responds in his own preoccupation with his mother, "You know she'd never commit suicide." And later at the climactic moment when Hickey explains that his wife has been killed—murdered, according to Larry—Parritt springs to his feet with, "You're a liar, Larry! . . . You know she's still alive!" Having revealed by this outburst that he considers himself to have been his mother's slayer, it is no use his insisting to Larry any longer, "It had nothing to do with her! It was just to get a few lousy dollars to blow in on a whore!"

Finally he drops all pretense when Hickey admits that he killed his dear Evelyn. "It's worse," Parritt exclaims, "if you kill someone and they have to go on living." He longs for death: "I'd be glad of the Chair!" is his cry. And no doubt, like some other murderers, it is self-destruction he has been seeking all the time. Hickey, at this point, is not happy to be a member of the same lodge as Parritt, although up to now he is the one who has insisted upon the association. But now he tells Larry: "get rid of that bastard. . . . There was love in my heart, not hate." Strangely enough, although each recognizes that the other was impelled by hate, he denies it in himself. Parritt now calls Hickey a liar, and protests concerning his mother, "I don't hate her!" But at the end of the play each abets the other's confession. When Hickey finds with surprise that he has torn up Evelyn's picture because he didn't "need it any more" (presumably he had subconsciously carried it to keep his hatred at fever pitch), Parritt in a "low insistent tone" confides: "I burnt up Mother's picture, Larry. Her eyes followed me all the time. They seemed to be wishing I was dead!" If it were not for the inappropriately sentimental tone of the poem, one might think of Oscar Wilde's "The Ballad of Reading Gaol": "Yet each man kills the thing he loves . . ./ The coward does it with a kiss,/ The brave man with a sword!"

As Hickey builds up to the truth through long narration, he reveals that the guilt he felt for his mistreatment of Evelyn was more than he could bear; when instead of taking a lover of her own or berating him, she merely kissed him with forgiveness, he felt that "it was like she did it on purpose to humiliate me, as if she'd spit in my face!" Knowing how unjust this accusation is, Hickey comes to loathe more and more the wife who thus makes

20

him doubly guilt-ridden. In *No Exit,* Garcin explains the situation between him and his wife: "Night after night I came home blind drunk, stinking of wine and women. She'd sat up for me, of course. But she never cried, never uttered a word of reproach. Only her eyes spoke. Big tragic eyes. . . . That woman was a martryr. . . ."[1] Garcin, who is at present in hell as a result of his past life, says that he regrets nothing. Hickey, likewise, claims at the end to feel no regret at having brought Evelyn the peace of death, but he too experiences a bit of hell as he realizes that he had really hated his wife for her martyr-like attitude towards his pursuit of a "piece" during life. Instead of continuing to boast about his murder, he claims insanity, and thus redeeming his listeners from death, saves himself from hell and goes courageously to death, whereas Garcin is shot down like a coward. "Hell is other people," especially people of the female variety. O'Neill might agree, for the result of their ravaging love is hell on this earth and martyrdom for them, and in a sense for their lovers as well, at the end of it.

Parritt, moved by Hickey's revelations and feeling the fire himself, actually confesses his hatred first: "I didn't give a damn about the money. It was because I hated her." In the next speech Hickey involuntarily reveals his detestation of Evelyn by calling her "damned bitch." Parritt claims to bear his hell more honestly than Hickey, whom he derides for putting up the "bluff" of pretending to be crazy for his defamation of Evelyn. He sticks to *his* "damned old bitch." Her refusal to let anyone but herself be free made killing her his only out. Hickey, too, could be free only if Evelyn was dead, but now free they are consumed in the fires of guilt.

In the case of the inhabitants of Hope's bar, there is no way for them to lessen their sense of guilt for the condition they are in—not only because they have botched their own lives but also because they have betrayed families who believed in them. It follows that their underlying desire for punishment is achieved by the increasing extremity of their failure. Atonement is a possible method of alleviating feelings of guilt, but there is no recompense that they are able to pay society or family; as to projecting any of their guilt upon others, this channel is not open either, for they are constrained to bless, not condemn, wife or mother. Although others may claim that Bessie was no paragon of sweet nature,

1. Jean-Paul Sartre, New York, 1958, p. 22.

only unconsciously do any words of reproach slip from Hope's mouth, and Hickey protests that Evelyn was angelic. Parritt may be critical of his mother but takes all the blame for the betrayal on himself. And assuredly none of the characters could believe that the one he has wronged really desired the wrong and hence brought it about. They are therefore mired in guilt for which they punish themselves. Their only solution is what R. D. Laing in *The Divided Self* calls one of "deliberate cultivation of a state of death-in-life as a defense against the pains of life."[2]

But they do save themselves from immediate death by the friendships engendered in the process of dream-sharing and drinking together. Besides the three prostitutes, there are no women characters in the play, but we learn of Parritt's mother (whom Larry loved), Hickey's wife, Hope's wife, and Jimmy Tomorrow's wife. Although we know least about the last, the affair between her and Jimmy fits the pattern of the others. Jimmy claims he took to drink because he found his wife in the hay with another man, but when Hickey challenges him, he finally admits that he was a drunkard long before that. "She soon found I much preferred drinking all night with my pals to being in bed with her." Unlike Hickey, he does not have to kill his wife because she—and he is grateful to her for it—gave him, as he puts it, "such a good tragic excuse to drink as much as I damned well pleased." The characters of the play bear out Karl Menninger's contention that "it is almost axiomatic that alcoholics in spite of a great show of heterosexual activity, have secretly a great fear of women and of heterosexuality in general."[3]

In the whole play there is no healthy or natural sex. Leslie Fiedler's thesis that the American novel reveals a tendency toward perversion and homosexuality in the American male is true of *The Iceman*. It is the camaraderie of the males in the barroom which alone gives evidence of warmth of human feeling. References to the absent or dead wives or mothers or lovers are foolishly sentimental or cold with hatred, and the only women characters in the play sell love to make their living. Fiedler's comment about Prew, the bugler, in James Jones' *From Here to Eternity*, applies to the men in Hope's bar. Prew learns "to know promotion and marriage and success as the lures that turn a man

2. Chicago, 1960, p. 151.
3. *Man Against Himself* (New York, 1938), p. 157.

from the purity of death—but especially to distrust marriage. To marry is to accept complicity, to recognize one's participation in universal guilt, for women do not know enough to die."[4] At the climax of the book Prew turns deliberately into a rain of machine-gun bullets, according to Fiedler, "to provide a fitting orgasm for the love that is death." On the other hand, in Hope's bar, devoid of threatening women, camaraderie prevails. There is much fun in the friendly banter, in the charges and countercharges of the males.

Although it probably cannot be equated here with the "latent homosexuality" which David Sievers sees as one of the "psychological *leit-motifs*"[5] throughout O'Neill's work, there is an "erotic component" in the relationship of the men upon which the "capacity for friendship" depends.[6] Piet Wetjoen (the General) and Cecil Lewis (the Captain) banter about the Boer War, affectionately charging each other with cowardice, while Hope's brother-in-law Ed Mosher and his friend, Pat McGloin, in a joking way complain about Bessie, who in Hope's view would put them out if she were alive. Even the Negro Joe is happily a member of the gang. When Lewis wakes from a drunken stupor, thinking he is still fighting the Boer War, and mistakes Joe for a "bloody Kaffir," he quickly apologizes with "Whitest colored man I ever knew," after Wetjoen points out that the black face at the table is that of "your old friend, Joe."

Willie Oban offers to take McGloin's case for reinstatement on the police force, and is just as anxious in a moment of consciousness to help Parritt, whom he believes the police are pursuing. At other times he pleads to be allowed to stay with his friends in the bar. "I'll go crazy alone!" he cries, when they threaten to bounce him upstairs. Although Hugo is made vicious by Hickey, his usual mood is "Vhy so serious, leedle monkey-faces? It's all great joke, no? So ve get drunk, and ve laugh like hell"—utterances usually greeted by good-humored jeering in the crowd. Jimmy Tomorrow is loved by the men because he outdoes them all in insisting that success will surely be his tomorrow. And Rocky and the girls, who might as well be male to judge by the lack of advances made to them by any character, have a very friendly

4. *An End to Innocence* (Boston, 1955), p. 188.
5. *Freud on Broadway* (New York, 1955), p. 132.
6. Menninger, p. 380.

23

relationship—completely unlike that of a pimp and his whores, as they keep insisting. "Dey like me. We're pals see?" says Rocky. Their attitude toward him is much like that of "two maternal, affectionate sisters toward a bullying brother whom they like to tease and spoil." The relationship of Chuck and Cora is something of the same, making their marriage as unlikely as the dreams of the other characters.

O'Neill explained to George Jean Nathan that "the dominant intention [of *The Iceman*] has been a study in the workings of strange friendship."[7] Even Hickey is entranced by the magic of Hope's bar. Just before he admits killing Evelyn, he tells the men that late at night after his wife had gone to bed, he would be wakeful: "I'd get so damned lonely. I'd get thinking how peaceful it was here, sitting around with the old gang, getting drunk and forgetting love. . . ." The preference of Jimmy and Hickey for the crowd at Hope's to their wives in bed testifies to a wonderful cohesion among the inhabitants of the bar which none of them shares with women. It is a companionship among fellow failures which provides at least a halfway exit from the hell of their lives and hence perhaps makes O'Neill slightly less pessimistic than Sartre. Hell is not other friendly male alcoholics.

Only Larry stands aside from the men and refuses to take part in their strange friendship. He may be lacking in erotic feeling as well, for Pearl and Margie kid him after he has called them his "great big beautiful baby dolls," insisting they are not his, though they are beautiful. "But what," Margie asks teasingly, "would he do wid beautiful dolls, even if he had de price, de old goat?" Then they accuse him of being "full of bull," which would seem to be a satirical pun on his lack of virility and its replacement with philosophizing, and in conjunction with the other animal epithet, a disparaging charge of lack of potency. Larry, apparently more stung than he likes to admit, responds by cursing Hickey with a vehemence which surprises the girls. But in any case, although Larry is accepted by the men, makes no attempt to reform them, and is drunk himself, he stands apart. He seems to have had an ardent sexual relationship with Parritt's mother, but cynicism has replaced warmth of feeling in him. "Leave what's dead in its grave," he says of his love for Rosa Parritt. He tries to kill even pity for any of the degenerates of the bar and at least pretends

7. *The Theatre Book of the Year 1946-1947*, p. 95.

to believe they would all be better off dead. His "erotic component" may be too weak for entering into human relationships. No matter how hard Parritt pursues him, pleading to be heard, Larry avoids or repulses the eighteen-year-old boy who looks to him as a father. He could have saved Parritt by giving a sympathetic ear to the young man's confession. As it is, he can see no solution but death for the conscience-stricken youth. Not that his coldness toward Parritt is so much greater than that toward everyone else, but it seems worse because the boy is in greater need of sympathy.

In times past Larry must have partaken of the warmth of the barroom: he throws a biting remark which hurts Hickey, who says, "We've always been good pals, haven't we? I know I've always liked you a lot," and Larry, "a bit shamefaced," replies, "Well, so have I liked you. Forget it, Hickey." But now, Larry, who is taken by critics to be the mouthpiece for O'Neill, is death-oriented like the playwright, who wrote to Barrett Clark, "I am sure that Man has definitely decided to destroy himself, and this seems to me the only truly wise decision he has ever made."[8] Larry says, "I've gotten beyond the desire to communicate with the world." He has reached the conclusion that the only thing better than death is not to have been born. And at the end he insists that Hickey has made him in reality that irrevocable convert to death which he has always claimed to be.

Larry and Hickey and Parritt, then, as the main characters, play out a drama of love and death against a no less anomalous background of guilt-stricken characters seeking death through drink. They are partly narcotized against the pain of life by the eroticism inherent in the companionship provided through the bottle as they drunkenly joke together about the iceman. He, to them all, is the bridegroom, encouraging a lusty but sardonic laugh which they sense is probably on themselves. O'Neill might have said, as Melville did, that the whole universe may be a "vast practical joke," the wit whereof man dimly discerns and more than suspects that it is "at nobody's expense but his own."[9] Willie Oban (who, like O'Neill himself, has become an alcoholic

8. Clark, *Eugene O'Neill: The Man and His Plays* (New York, 1947), p. 145.
9. Herman Melville, *Moby Dick* (New York: Signet Classics, 1961), p. 225.

812.52
D58j

after an interval at an ivy league college where he was not socially acceptable) takes this attitude while waiting for "Hickey or Death" to come. He feels great resentment toward his father and has caused his mother, who for years has tried to cure him, to abandon him forever. Since he is said to be "Knocking on the door" of hell when the play opens, he is perhaps closer than any of the others to physical demise. He appears to welcome self-destruction and actually to prefer Death to Hickey, the iceman-joke-teller and booze-bringer. Meanwhile he sings a bawdy ballad concerning a fair maiden upon whose door a sailor (or iceman in Oban's version) gives three lusty knocks. It is in line with O'Neill's inferential use of language throughout the play that he intends a relationship between the coarse expression "knocked up," as it might apply to the maid in the ballad, and Oban's raps upon the table, which represents the gate of hell as well as the girl's door. No doubt O'Neill also knew the joke about Billy Sunday's admonition to the girls in the front row: Draw your knees together and keep the gates of Hell closed.

Even in minor details of characterization and language, O'Neill carries out with sardonic humor what he called the "death double meaning" of the title.[10] One wonders if, as a boy, having been early introduced to the lewd by his older brother, he did not add in a whisper, "between the sheets," when he heard the reading: "Lo, the bridegroom cometh." Shortly after the completion of the play and six years before its production, he wrote to George Jean Nathan: "Well, I hope you like 'The Iceman Cometh.' Including the title, which I love, because it characteristically expresses so much of the outer and the inner spirit of the play." O'Neill had a right to "admire this opus," for it is, as he claimed, "as successful an attempt at accomplishing a thing comprehensively and completely in all aspects as I've ever made."[11] And so, carrying out the iceman-bridegroom theme, the men of Hope's bar, at the end, accept the death—real or symbolic—of Parritt, Hickey, and Larry, and cynically await their own with jeering laughter and bawdy song.

O'Neill had spent three decades in envisioning the central

10. Letter to George Jean Nathan from Tao House, August 30, 1940. Quoted by permission of Carlotta O'Neill through Donald Gallup, Curator, Eugene O'Neill Collection, Yale University Library.

11. Letter to George Jean Nathan from Tao House, February 8, 1940. Quoted by permission.

metaphor of the play. In previous plays he struggled with concepts concerning the nature of love, human and divine, and the relationship of love to death. Edwin Engel believes that "for forty years O'Neill had been obsessed with death, and at last had come to terms with it" in *The Iceman Cometh*.[12] The terms he came to are that man is "a mixture of mud and manure," and that love is a dirty joke told by men to men and resulting in death. O'Neill, who as Edmund in the autobiographical play *Long Day's Journey into Night* is always "a little in love with death," was, when he wrote *The Iceman*, unequivocally committed to it. As Norman Chaitin notes, "O'Neill lived all his life with death in his body. Death was with him all the time, inside him."[13] Lying in a hospital for six months with tuberculosis impressed upon him his nearness to it. He tried to escape by drink, and tried to escape by the affirmation in a play like *Lazarus Laughed* that there is no death, but nothing worked, so with smutty laughter at the world, in *The Iceman Cometh*, he despaired.

In the terrible pre-World-War-II years, the frightening truth that men enjoy killing and would not admire war if all weapons were non-lethal seemed more and more evident to the playwright and brought him more and more disillusionment. Twenty-five years earlier he had loved to recite Thompson's "The Hound of Heaven" in the Hell Hole, and had done it so effectively that a friend, Dorothy Day, had been moved to take stock of her whole life, become a Catholic, and establish a settlement house on the Bowery.[14] Although O'Neill would no doubt have considered this the wrong kind of pity, he apparently believed that God pursues man with holy love. However, according to Dorothy Day, even then O'Neill "was absorbed by death and darkness," and in her opinion considered his drinking as a rehearsal for his death. She heard him recite from memory and with intense feeling Thompson's "To the Dead Cardinal of Westminister":

> Life is coquetry
> Of death, which wearies me,
> Too sure
> Of the amour;

12. "O'Neill, 1960," *Modern Drama*, III, 3 (Dec., 1960), 222.
13. "O'Neill: The Power of Daring," *Modern Drama*, III, 3 (Dec., 1960), 233.
14. Croswell Bowen with the assistance of Shane O'Neill, *The Curse of the Misbegotten* (New York, 1959), p. 96.

A tiring-room where I
Death's divers garments try
Till fit
Some fashions sit.

It seemeth me too much
I do rehearse for such
A mean
And single scene.[15]

The metaphor is one which might well appeal to a young man
with a knowledge of the theater, and the theme that the amour
with death is too sure to require a lifetime of coquetry accorded
with the sometime mood of the young playwright. If life is merely
a rehearsal for the love-death, the performance of which doesn't
warrant such lengthy pains, then the ambiguity of existence makes
life nothing but coquetry, and death an end and final performance to be highly desired.

All of this O'Neill felt with even greater cynicism when he
wrote *The Iceman,* although the title was apparently even then
revolving in his mind, for the only words he passed with Agnes
Boulton at a party were, "It's a cold night—good night for a party.
The iceman cometh."[16] And during the next two decades he wrote
various plays which contributed to his masterpiece of 1939. One
of these was an adaptation of Coleridge's *The Ancient Mariner*
for the Provincetown Playhouse, the theme of which—the evil-
doer driven to relate his tale as expiation for his crime—is an
important one in *The Iceman.* In O'Neill's play two characters
are in this position: Parritt tries to make confession of the betrayal of his mother to Larry, who refuses to listen, and Hickey
seeks expiation for the murder of his wife by relating his story
at length to the whole gang, who likewise are unappreciative
listeners.

In the case of Parritt, confession might save his sanity, but
Larry repeatedly refuses to play the part of priest, and Parritt
is driven to suicide. When O'Neill in 1912 lived at the water-
front dive called Jimmy the Priest's, a roommate committed suicide by jumping out of the window. O'Neill has given Larry some
of the characteristics of the proprietor, who had "mild blue eyes"

15. Gelb, *O'Neill,* p. 360.
16. Bowen, p. 96.

28

with the quality of a "pitying but weary old priest's," but Larry's eyes have as well "a gleam of sharp sardonic humor." Larry may also be modeled on Terry Carlin, a friend from the Hell Hole days of 1917, who gave a distraught alcoholic a lethal dose of heroin.[17] This incident too haunted O'Neill, who may have seen himself in the part of Larry, actually encouraging Parritt to die. In Coleridge's poem, the wedding guest, who instead of partaking of the marriage feast must listen to the mariner's tale, turns at the end from the bridegroom and the sounds of merriment, even though he is "next of kin," a "sadder and wiser" man. In his heart, and perhaps in O'Neill's, remains the vision of "The Nightmare Life-in-Death . . . who thicks man's blood with cold."

Hickey, as much as Parritt, although perhaps not so obviously, feels the need of absolution through lengthy expatiation on his story. He prolongs the climax of his tale, as does the ancient mariner, in order to insure the attention of his listeners. On the first morning he reveals nothing of Evelyn's death; that night, merely that she is dead; on the following morning, that she has been murdered; and late the next night, that he is the slayer. Like the ancient mariner, who first suffers "evil looks" from the crew and then more horrible, the curse of their dead eyes, Hickey pleads at the end, "It makes me feel like hell to think you hate me." He expects expiation from his confession and instead receives only hatred, for he has shot the albatross of their daydreams, and he says, "It makes me feel you suspect I must have hated you." And indeed the purpose of his visit to the hell-hole was, at least unconsciously, hatred for life, not love of it. As Larry insists, "I felt he'd brought the touch of death on him."

As the bodies of the sailors drop dead "one by one" in front of the mariner's eyes, under the influence of the specter-bark on which Death sails, so each man becomes death-like under Hickey's prodding. "The curse in a dead man's eye" brings torture to the mariner, which is finally relieved by his blessing the least of God's creatures, the watersnakes. So Hickey lifts the curse by claiming insanity—"I'd gone insane. . . . I've been out of my mind ever since"—as the men in a friendly "chorus of eager assent" shout, "We knew he was crazy!" Jibes at the detectives, who doubt the insanity plea, include Hope's "Bejees, you know the old story, when Saint Patrick drove the snakes out of Ireland they swam to

17. Gelb, p. 367.

New York and joined the police force." The sympathy for Hickey is reinforced by an encouraging chorus, "They can't give you the chair. We'll testify you was crazy." His story has not made the men sadder and wiser, but its disavowal has removed the curse of their hatred from Hickey. It is as if the albatross had been revived, and the booze again has a kick to it.

It is pertinent that in O'Neill's dramatic version of *The Ancient Mariner,* the bride and groom, glimpsed for a moment on the stage, are like puppets and the guests mere dancing shadows on a window blind. This bride and groom are spiritually dead. The iceman of dull Philistinism has cast his cold hand on the festivities, which ring with falsity, in contrast to the old mariner's words which ring with truth. Death, masked in a black skull, who appears during the mariner's narration, is more vivid and alive than are the celebrants, and so are the masked shipmates who appear as drowned men and later as angels. The solid reality of the men in *The Iceman* would make masks inappropriate, for, as John Gassner says, the characters are "fleshed out" and "come alive as fully realized persons."[18] But the marriages and love affairs of the play, which we learn about in falsely sentimentalized memories, bear a striking resemblance to shadows on a window blind.

With his magnificent sense of the sardonic, O'Neill has Chuck and Cora dressed up for their wedding almost like puppets—Chuck in a straw hat with a flashy band and a Sunday-best blue suit with high stiff collar, and Cora in her gaudy best, her face plastered with rouge and mascara—and tops the ridiculous picture with Rocky's line, "Pipe de bridegroom, Larry! All dolled up for de killin'!" As an echo of the title in reverse, it reiterates the theme of the play: the bridegroom goeth—to death. Thus, in Tennessee Williams' *Period of Adjustment,* the newlyweds set out in a hearse. Cora asks, "Say, why don't all you barflies come to de weddin'?" But the only response, even to Cora's prodding, is Rocky's, "Here's hopin' yuh don't moider each odder before next week." And after they have left, his epitaph for them is, "One regular guy and one all-right tart gone to hell!" Hell is hot and the iceman of death is cold; so is lust hot and its aftermath of hatred cold. The bridegroom, warm and loving, is piped on for the cold killing.

18. "The Playwright and the Contemporary World," *Theatre Arts,* XLVIII, 1 (Jan., 1964), 72.

The ambiguity between love and death, no matter how O'Neill views it, always defies definition. As Doris Falk notes, "In the last plays O'Neill walked in the valley not of death alone, but of nothingness in which all values are illusions and all meaning fades before the terror of ambiguity."[19] Only Larry profits by Hickey's tale of horror, but he is perhaps as badly off as the unenlightened guests at the wedding or as the men in Hope's bar, because he is in the ambiguous position of really believing now that death is the best solution, but of being unable to die. But, as Doris Falk further explains, "His very inability to propel himself actively toward this annihilation—to accomplish it through suicide—is also death . . . he is not even a paralyzed spectator; he is dead."[20] If, as in *The Ancient Mariner*, Death and Life-in-Death were dicing for the souls of the men, Larry's would be won by the latter.

Of course there is ambiguity in the parable that Jesus, the bridegroom, is inviting the virgins whose lamps are burning to join him in death, which is nevertheless love everlasting and life eternal. And there is ambiguity in the moral of *The Ancient Mariner* that love in the heart is born of terror and that the guest learns more of it from the ancient mariner than from the wedding festivities. O'Neill in his dramatic version adds a further ambiguity at the end. As the mariner pronounces the moral—"He prayeth well who loveth well"—and blesses the audience while crossing himself, the wedding guest, instead of turning "from the bridegroom's door . . . a sadder and wiser man," as in the poem, bolts into the house "as if running from the dark" and later appears in shadow on the blind, dancing with the bride as music rises in the background. He apparently renounces the message and turns to false merriment as he "shuts and bolts" the door, or else fearing the message, avoids enlightenment in embracing the bride.

Larry, who plays the part of the wedding guest to Parritt more specifically than to Hickey, is in the strange position of being brought to the point of urging Parritt and even Hickey to death, but of being unable to will his own. He bolts from his position of death-lover, as if running from the dark, and is unable to join the death-dance at Hope's bar. Parritt has felt about Larry, like the

19. *Eugene O'Neill and the Tragic Tension* (New Brunswick, N. J., 1958), p. 201.
20. Page 162.

ancient mariner about the wedding guest: "The moment that his face I see,/ I know the man that must hear me:/ To him my tale I teach." Parritt and Hickey parallel each other in their recitals, but nobody at Hope's party except the tellers profits by the tales, unless it might be said that Larry profits too much by conversion to death. So ambiguity is piled on ambiguity. The conclusion is fitting for the title. Whatever kind of love it is that has united Hope and Bessie, Jimmy and Marjorie, Larry and Rosa Parritt, Hickey and Evelyn, and even Chuck and Cora, it is not fruitful and leads to "de killin'" and not to the praying which means spiritual acceptance of life. The human heart is frozen into numbness, as the ship upon which the ancient mariner sails is frozen in the sea. In O'Neill's dramatic version of the poem, various instruments were used to make the sound of the ice, which "crack'd and growl'd, and rear'd and howl'd,/ Like noises in a swound!" The play perhaps remained vivid in the memory of the playwright, who thought of revising it for the Federal Theater in 1937,[21] two years before he completed *The Iceman Cometh*.

Using more Christian symbolism than Coleridge does, O'Neill's stage directions make the albatross appear "like a huge Dove of the Holy Ghost," to whom the sailors offer bread which is "like Communion wafers," and the sunlight which melts the ice with its warmth is made to appear to flood down from the albatross like a holy light. There is no doubt—even if he had not been so explicit later in *Days Without End*—that O'Neill would have liked to believe in life eternal and a heavenly marriage with Christ. But like the wedding guest at the end of the staged version of the poem, he bolts from the message of Mother Church back into the shadowy world of celebration of erotic love which is death. One is reminded of the hero's contention in *The Snows of Kilimanjaro:* "Love is a dunghill. And I'm the cock that gets on it to crow."

Rather than imposing a philosophical meaning upon life, where none exists for them, the characters of *The Iceman* retain a juvenile dependency upon dreams and drink and survive upon the masochistic joke that sex is the iceman of death which will get them in the end. The sterility of their lives—emphasized by the absence of normal women as characters in the play—is underlined even more fully by the lack of mention of children born to

21. Donald Gallup (ed.), "Eugene O'Neill's 'The Ancient Mariner,'" *Yale University Library Gazette*, XXXV (Oct., 1960), 61-86.

any of the women they have loved. If the climax of love—even though it mean death—results in procreation, life in the race survives. But in a world without progeny, death is the end of the race as well as of the individual. James Joyce saw something of the ambiguity of the love-death between Anna Livia Plurabelle and H. C. Earwicker, but at least H.C.E. stands for Haveth Childers Everywhere, whereas in *The Iceman* the characters can ward off despair only through the hope of their pipe dreams.[22]

22. Pointing out that love "crucifies" with "no resurrection" in the play, Robert J. Andreach explains the women of the play as inverted figures of the Virgin Mary: The names Cora, Margie, Pearl, Bessie, Rosa, Marjorie, and Molly refer to the Virgin in various ways, as does the name Evelyn to Eve, the old Mary—"O'Neill's Women in *The Iceman Cometh*," *Renascence*, XVIII, 2 (Winter, 1966), 89-98.

3. ACTION

Like the setting and the characters, the action of *The Iceman* reinforces the theme of the love of death. The form and content of the play are therefore one: the meaning is conveyed in a unique structure by the only possible characters in the most appropriate setting. To put it another way, changes in any of the three would change not only the form of the play but its content. As John Ciardi advises not to ask *what* but *how* a poem means, so one should examine O'Neill's play to see how the structure of the action works to convey the theme. Francis Fergusson has pointed out that although action and plot are different, experts in the field of dramatic theory have difficulty in defining and separating them; but it is possible to say about any given play what the object of the action is. For example, in *Oedipus Rex* the object of the action is to find the culprit and the structure of the play evolves from the pursuit of this object.[1] In *The Iceman* the object of the action—euphemistically put—is to find peace.

This may be said to be the object of the drunks and of Hickey as well, and it is also the object of Hickey in regard to the drunks. But the peace experienced by Hickey, who hoped to find it through love, is that of death. And the peace which Hickey brings the men, as Larry says, is "the peace of death." Even though, with Hickey's departure, they recover some joy of life through the bottle, by this very means they are well advanced on the road to peace through death. In the language, in the setting, and in the action of the characters, the playwright emphasizes that it is the peace of death which all seek, and the title reinforces the submerged object of the action—to find love in death and death in love.

Critics of the play have noted two intertwining themes: that man needs illusions in order to survive and that love is really hate. Edwin Engel sees the second as of most importance. "The unmasking of love," he says, "is the main intention of the play." He further believes that "love, illicit or otherwise, has been converted into its contrary, death."[2] Engel is correct in pointing out

1. *The Idea of a Theater* (Princeton, 1949), p. 230.
2. *The Haunted Heroes of Eugene O'Neill* (Cambridge, Mass., 1953), p. 294.

34

the main intention of the play, as is Eric Bentley in noting that the truth-illusion theme is a red herring over the trail of the love-hate theme.[3] But both assume, as is usually done, that love and death are contraries, or that love and hate are opposites, whereas the great truth at which O'Neill arrives is that psychologically and physiologically they result in the same thing. Life may be said to be one big copulation—a joke that goes on between womb and tomb—until in one final agony or spasm the iceman cometh and man relaxes into the peace of death. The lover kills his mistress and dies. The phallic connotations of weapons are deep in mythology. According to the dying Cleopatra, "The stroke of death is as a lover's pinch/ Which hurts and is desired." And early in the play Enobarbus makes the suggestive remark to Antony about the passionate queen, "I do think there is mettle in death which commits some loving act upon her, she hath such a celerity in dying."[4] Of course sex was born with death, when Adam and Eve knew "carnal desire" and ceased to be immortal at the time of the fall. Again, sex in the form of the snake is the villain that brought them death. When new life is created, it is necessary that the old should die, so the subconscious correlation between death and love has a basis in biology. As Brigid Brophy says, "The unconscious has an inevitable biological foundation for the equation it is constantly making between sexual penetration and penetration with a weapon, between imposing or suffering an orgasm and imposing or suffering death."[5] Engel combines the illusion and love themes by restating his idea of the play: "Out of the unmasking, one truth, together with its corollary, emerges above all others: love is an illusion, and all women are bitches or whores."[6] He might well have gone on to say that all love is bitching and whoring, the wages of which are death, rather than, as he does, that "love is non-existent" in *The Iceman Cometh*. It does exist and motivates the main action of the play, but it exists in ribald iceman jokes about the lustful lover who is death.

It would be going too far to say that *The Iceman* is purposely structured in detail in the pattern of sexual intercourse, but the rhythmic movement of the action, the repetitious back-and-forth

3. *In Search of Theater* (New York, 1953), p. 242.
4. Shakespeare, *Antony and Cleopatra*, V.ii and I.ii.
5. *Black Ship to Hell* (New York, 1962), p. 45.
6. *Haunted Heroes*, p. 286.

35

reactions which Hickey brings out in the characters, their re-
solves one by one to go and face the world, their return defeated,
their charges upon Hickey one after another, and their final re-
laxation in song at the end, will be shown to have something of
the erotic "coming" of the iceman. The structure is by no means
obvious and has even appeared haphazard to critics, but José
Quintero, after directing the play, insists that those who find
it "rambling and overwritten" have missed its complete precision
of form. To an actor in the original production who complained
that O'Neill had made the same point eighteen times, O'Neill
replied, "I intended it to be repeated eighteen times."[7] And on the
front page of the manuscript, he wrote to Lawrence Langner,
"To hell with your cuts!"[8] The structure of the action, therefore,
needs further analysis.

A play in which ten characters sit through an exceedingly long
first act without moving is unusual—probably unique. Besides this,
five other characters merely enter and sit. It has been suggested,
in view of the quantities of red-eye they are consuming, that
some might use the "This is it," which juts out in the left rear
corner, and Piet Wetjoen would seem the obvious candidate. But
the fifteen remain glued to their chairs, pacifically except in
instances when Hugo rolls around mouthing his anarchistic jargon and Willie Oban rises slightly to sing his rap-rap-rap ballad.
Besides Parritt, who enters early, and the prostitutes, who enter
at dawn, no one moves except the two bartenders, who are about
to change shifts. The whole long act seems preparation for Hickey's entrance, which comes near its end. With all eyes on him he
makes what would seem to be the traditional grand stage entrance, forecasting a change of pace and much stage movement.
But although the men greet him with "affectionate acclaim," he
merely passes quickly around shaking hands, then sits at an empty
table and remains in his chair until the end of the act. The stage
director, once he has the tables well placed, is not troubled by
one character's covering another or mistiming a crossing.

It wasn't because O'Neill didn't know theater that he wrote
the first act without stage movement and insisted upon its being
played as he wrote it, but because he wished to portray a world
in the valley of the shadow of death. Expectations of Hickey's

7. Bowen, p. 308.
8. Langner, *The Magic Curtain* (New York, 1951), p. 406.

bringing balm in the form of iceman jokes and further torpor in the form of liquor are dashed by Hickey's attempt to get a Reform Wave going. But even with his enthusiasm for the project, the tomb-like atmosphere of the place also prevails on him as he settles down in a chair for a long snooze. "Don't let me be a wet blanket," he repeats shortly after his entrance and again as the curtain falls, but a wet blanket he is, more than wet enough to smother the slight flames of spirit which were fanned briefly by his entrance.

In spite of the lack of stage movement, tension rises throughout the act, because of the expectancy with which the men await Hickey's arrival. As in *Waiting for Lefty* and in *Waiting for Godot*, the agony is prolonged and intense.[9] "Would that Hickey or death would come!" is a call of which the audience more and more feels the immediacy. Like most awaited events, Hickey's arrival is a long time coming, and an exceeding disappointment when it does come. As part of the buildup toward the climax of the love-death, it is a frost, because its tense, slow rise is unrewarded. Hickey adds a bit of jazz when, not long after his arrival, he peels off a ten-spot and orders Rocky: "Keep the balls coming until this is killed." The old Hickey is recognizable to Hope in this remark, but his refusal to help kill the booze and his continued jabbing at their pipe dreams dampen everyone's spirits, and as the curtain falls they all stare resentfully at the dozing Hickey.

9. Two other important plays of the twentieth century are, like Act I of *The Iceman*, waiting plays: Clifford Odets' *Waiting for Lefty* (1935) and Samuel Beckett's *Waiting for Godot* (1953). Actually, since Act I of *The Iceman* is so long, the waiting for Hickey consumes perhaps as much time as does the waiting for Lefty or for Godot. In Odets' proletarian drama of the depression years, Lefty never shows up by reason of having been shot in the head behind the taxicab barns, but the exploited hacks take courage from his death, and declaring themselves "stormbirds of the working-class," call a strike against the cab companies. With victorious shouts of "Strike! Strike!" in which the audience engages, the workers become heroes who will suffer and die to make a new world. By way of contrast, Estragon and Vladimir quietly wait beside a bare road for two days during two repetitious acts, with the sole purpose of meeting Godot, who never comes because he is delayed until the next day, or perhaps because he does not exist.

O'Neill's play partakes more of the pessimistic tone of the latter, but more of the dramatic technique of the former. The tomorrow-dreams of the men correspond to the tramps' expectations of Godot's arrival on each morrow, and Godot is perhaps as much an illusion as is love to O'Neill's bums. But the grouped men in *The Iceman* and in *Waiting for Lefty* make similar choric responses to the question "Where de hell's Hickey?" or, in regard to

The first act, of course, does cover a certain amount of necessary exposition, but as cut-prone directors have complained, it covers it numerous times and at much greater length than necessary to get the information across—even to the densest audience. O'Neill's purpose is not to get on with the show but to protract it. When, after a long night of waiting, Lo, the bridegroom cometh (for Hickey, like the bridegroom in Matthew, had tarried), the irony is not that all do not have oil for their lamps, but that the bridegroom has not been worth waiting for. Instead of the foolish virgins being left outside the door with the Lord saying, "I know you not," Hickey calls all to find peace, but they are all reluctant. No one wishes to proceed with him to the marriage feast of reality. Hickey, instead of warning the alcohol-soaked bums, "Ye know not the day nor the hour," chides, "The hour is today." When one does not know the hour, it is always tomorrow, but "the great Nihilist" brings death with him to the feast, and the hour has struck. Nor is there resurrection as the bride of Christ, although Mosher, who has been least taken in by Hickey's sermon, does relate at the close of the act that a doctor friend of his "claimed that rattlesnake oil, rubbed on the prat, would cure heart failure in three days." Thus, perhaps, One rose from the tomb? Later, in another of the paradoxical juxtapositions in which the

---

Lefty, "Where the hell did he disappear?" Of course, the chanting "We want Lefty! Lefty! Lefty!" results in disappointment, whereas Hickey's arrival is greeted by a unison of affectionate acclaim. Ironically enough, however, Lefty's death brings the workers to life, whereas Hickey's arrival carries the drunks to the edge of death. The technique of reviewing the past lives of the characters, which Odets does in staged flashbacks, O'Neill does by verbal reminiscence. Neither shows traditional dramaturgy, but it can be said of *The Iceman*, as R. Baird Shuman says of *Waiting for Lefty*, "The customary devices used to develop a play structurally are not necessary"— *Clifford Odets* (New York, 1962), p. 53.

Chronologically, O'Neill's play comes between Odets' and Beckett's. It reflects the pessimism of the early days of World War II, and complete disillusionment with Odets' idea that social organizations can resolve man's ills, but it barely skirts the concern which Beckett shows for man's existential condition, and purveys a deeper despair.

It is also interesting to note, in view of the waiting-for-the-bridegroom parable, that O'Neill wrote a short story, "Tomorrow" (*The Seven Arts*, June, 1917) about the character called Jimmy Tomorrow, whom he later used in *The Iceman*, and that the first-person narrator, Jimmy's roommate, is waiting in their dingy room above the bar for this procrastinating character to bring oil for the lamp which is slowly sputtering out and leaving him in darkness.

play abounds, Larry points out that Hickey has "the miraculous touch to raise the dead," for he has started the Boer War raging again between Lewis and Wetjoen.

Like a bridegroom, or an iceman, playing it cool, O'Neill, then, while laying the groundwork for Hickey's suit, deliberately thwarts overt action, and although ever increasing the tension, prevents normal release, so that at close of Act I the inhabitants of Hope's bar sit in bewildered suspense. In the opening speeches between Larry and Rocky the playwright has explained almost everything about this palace of pipe dreams, which he then takes an entire lengthy act to illustrate case by case. He also makes Larry, for Parritt's benefit, describe each character, and makes Hickey's arrival the cause of another review of each case. There is a purposefully annoying repetition of the theme of illusion as seen in each character throughout the act. And the truth about each—even Larry himself—is to be found at once if the audience is perceptive enough in diagnosing the charges and countercharges, but it too lives in a world of illusion, and so it is only the surface truth which the audience sees. For the ultimate truth, it must wait through four acts of slow, deliberate wooing.

Repetition is the essence of Act I: Rocky knocks Larry's dream and Larry replies; Hugo knocks Rocky's dream and Rocky replies; Rocky complains about Hope and Hope replies; Larry is accused of being a friend of Parritt's and he replies; Joe accuses Parritt of having money and Parritt replies; Parritt accuses Larry of loving his mother and the Movement and Larry replies; Hugo accuses Parritt of being a stool pigeon and Parritt replies. Larry then describes the drunks, and several other characters berate each other. Then the illusions of the characters are exposed: Jimmy takes to dreaming, Joe takes to dreaming, Hope takes to dreaming, Lewis and Wetjoen take to dreaming, Willie takes to dreaming, McGloin and Mosher take to dreaming. As dawn comes, the streetwalkers enter, dreaming with Rocky that they are "good kids" and that he is a bartender. Chuck and Cora enter dreaming. Hickey, now a teetotaler who has found peace, enters and stops the dreaming. He first takes Hope as "an example," then Jimmy, then Larry, then Parritt, and each of the others in turn. Except for the bit of merriment which Mosher manages to create at the end, all joy is extinguished by wet-blanket Hickey as the curtain falls.

At the opening of Act II the girls and bartenders, observed by Larry, are making preparations for Hope's birthday party. This festive Last Supper with seventeen at the table should result also, through the quantities of champagne which Hickey provides, in a Dionysian orgy of primitive proportions; but under Hickey's lugubrious influence the wine fails to take effect, and rather than a yea-saying paganism, a Puritan nay-saying prevails. The pleasant goading between characters becomes malicious and bitter. As Hickey prods them toward self-recognition, they turn with fright and despair upon one another. The disturbing influence of mind has destroyed jubilation of spirit. The meddler has depressed the *joie de vivre* by his insistence upon meaning in life. The unification which the God Pan inspires is dead, and the revel never gets off the ground. In the context of the Last Supper or of a bridal supper, the celebration is also a failure. The wine is not consecrated, and does not represent resurrection. It is tainted by this-worldly reality, which Hickey claims will bring eternal peace, but Hickey is a secular savior, who the men recognize is selling the wrong kind of peace. This is not to imply, however, that Christ the bridegroom brings the right kind. That kind also is a pipe dream. It may be suitable for some, but it is dreaming which ends in sure death. Dionysus or Christ may be resurrected in ritual, but at the end of Act II it is certain that Hickey's wife, Evelyn, will never be.

The rhythmic motion of the second act begins with Hickey's reform wave in full swing. The angered characters engage in oral charges and, now, even physical encounters with the monotonous repetition of Act I. Cora and Pearl fly at each other. Rocky slaps Margie. Hugo curses Hickey for making him mock the Movement. Joe turns sullen and gets called nigger and coon. Larry swears at Hickey for his meddling and Parritt for his pursuit. Willie comes in "sick and haunted." Parritt stings Larry with, "You old bastard, you'll never die as long as there's a free drink of whiskey left." Lewis and Wetjoen come to bodily blows. Mosher and McGloin after a series of insults pull back their fists to fight. Jimmy, "obviously frightened," shrinks back into himself. Hope yells to the gang to cut out the noise, hurts the three girls into tears, and later berates the whole gang. This hate-wave appearing in the beloved proprietor and honoree of the evening is shattering to them all. Only his relenting, "Bejees, you know

40

you're all as welcome here as the flowers in May," saves them from misery. The act nears its close with a kind of anomalous hurting and healing, anger and reconciliation, love and hate, which extends even to Hickey.

As Larry taunts Hickey about his wife and the iceman, the others break into jeering laughter, but Hickey's announcement that Evelyn is dead brings contrite murmurs of, "Forgive me, Hickey," "Sorry, Hickey," "We're sorry, Hickey." But the wave rolls halfway back again as Hickey proclaims that he feels joy, not grief, and the emotion of the men as the curtain falls is one of "bewildered, incredulous confusion." A strange feeling of friendship which includes Hickey has momentarily prevailed, but Hickey's protest, in the same metaphor he has used at the end of Act I, that Evelyn's death must not be a wet blanket on the proceedings, goes unheeded. Unlike the wet blanket which covers the iceman's shoulder to provide protection, Hickey, the wooer, seems either deliberately or inadvertently to use it to quench the sympathetic love which is striving to burst into flame.

At the beginning of Act III Rocky explains that Hickey has been pursuing the gang "from room to room all night." "He's got his Reform Wave goin' strong dis mornin'," says the barman. With almost orgiastic fury Hickey has dragged Jimmy out to get his laundry, sent Willie with the money to buy his clothes back, and forced all the rest to shave and brush in spite of the shakes. He has maddened Parritt, dismayed Larry, and made the old anarchist Hugo almost mad. He has brought Chuck and Rocky to blows. He listens to their plans for the day and forces them out: first Joe, then Cora and Chuck, then Lewis and Wetjoen, then Mosher and McGloin, then Willie, then Jimmy, and finally Hope. Of course it is only a few moments after Hope, enraged by Hickey, has dashed out across the street that he returns claiming a car had almost hit him. And it might as well have been true because to Hugo, Hope "looks dead."

The immense wave which has carried the bums into the world of reality will bring them back in the undertow—sadder but wiser men, according to Hickey's calculations. But the peace of death which he has brought them proves that they have drowned in the process. Unlike Acts I and II which end in frustration and resentment, Act III ends climactically. The pace of the rhythm has increased throughout the act, with one character after another

41

leaving the Hell Hole at shorter and shorter intervals until only Rocky at the bar, Hugo stupefied at one table, and Parritt, Larry, and Hickey are left. When Hope charges back inside, looking like death, Hugo sees "blood beneath the willow trees," Parritt admits to the betrayal of his mother, and Larry echoes shakenly that Evelyn was murdered—no doubt remains that Hickey is the death-bringing bridegroom. His denials mean nothing. As far as the men are concerned, he has successfully brought them to the point of death.

At the beginning of Act IV, all are drained of life. "Licked," with illusions gone, they submit to that reality which is death. Joe admits to being a "damned nigger," Rocky and Chuck that they are pimps, Lewis that he is honored that a black man would sit next to him. Parritt is trying to make "stew-bum" Larry his executioner. Chuck wants to kill Hickey, and all agree with Rocky that they might as well take a hop off the fire escape. "What de hell's de difference? Who cares?" they mutter with numbed minds. And later in a "dull complaining chorus," they expostulate, "We can't pass out! You promised us peace!" The death which Hickey has brought is not the exhausted drunken sleep of the Dionysian reveler, who having consumed the old God, knows a new will rise with the next grape harvest. Hickey has driven hard to his end, and to a man, all have responded to his advances, but frustration rather than peace has been the result. And he can arouse them no more. His frantic appeal, "You're my old pals, the only friends I've got," is met with sodden silence. They have been courted for the last time; somehow Hickey has failed to bring it off. He is "breathin' hard" in Act IV, but not inducing the company any closer to a cohesive response to his obsession.

The choric reactions to Hickey's speeches in Act IV come with ritual-like regularity. Sometimes one character is the leader, as when Chuck proclaims, "All we want outa you is keep de hell away from us and give us a rest," and the chorus mutters assent. But sometimes all speak together, as a united chorus, as when they pound glasses on the table and chant, "Who the hell cares? We want to pass out!" All will stage a celebration "when dat bastard goes to de Chair," as Rocky shouts. And although Hickey tries to explain, "There was love in my heart, not hate," the men deride him. It is not love they want, not that serious thrust of love which Hickey has brought, not that elevating, ecstatic love whose end is bound to be death. They want that fun and laughter which is life. Larry pleads with Hickey for the old times, "when you brought kindness and laughter with you instead of death." And Chuck points out that, although it was silly for him to think of marrying Cora, still, "it was fun, kinda, me and Cora kiddin' ourselves." Laughter and fun are missing from the love which Hickey brings.

As he approaches the climax of his long speech, the hypnotic effect overcomes even the two detectives. The chorus has punctuated the speech from time to time with "What's it to us? All we want is to pass out in peace," like "sleepers who curse a person who keeps awakening them." Near the final confession, when Hickey is looking for Evelyn's picture, "the silence is like that in the room of a dying man where people hold their breath, waiting for him to die." The men have reached the point of death already. Hickey's ecstasy is still to come, so they wait, hardly breathing themselves, for him to die. As the tension builds up, Hope leads the chorus, "Give us a rest, for the love of Christ," which all take up to the clamor of banging glasses. The chanting gives the cry an almost religious fervor. Upon the climactic words, "I killed her," it is Parritt who experiences the orgasm, who relaxes limply in his chair with a "strange exhausted relief." From near the beginning of the play, he has been hanging between life and death, but now he is committed, and needs only Larry's words, "Get the hell out of life," to make the intellectual decision which has already been made for him emotionally.

As for Hickey, he comes almost to the point of death, but his rhythm is broken by the shock of his cursing Evelyn, and he "stops with a horrified start." His self-revelation of the truth that he killed Evelyn because he hated her destroys his erotic impetus. He turns pleadingly to the men—"Boys, you're all my old pals!" —for the first time not the doughty wooer, but the impotent failure. To have been brought so near the point of climax and then to be frustrated leaves him no response but the plea of insanity. Unexpectedly and ironically, it is this plea which revives the others, and which they eagerly insist upon, in spite of his momentary impulse to deny it. As he is taken off "to spill his guts" at the police station, he cries, "I want to go to the Chair," and there he will find consummation. Ironically enough

43

also, it is his death which brings life to the men as the death of the Wine God or the Christian God does to the believer. Finally Larry, whose tight-shut eyes frighten the men, is brought to the point of death while waiting in agony for Parritt's leap from the fire escape. At the sound of the hurtling body hitting the ground, "he gasps and drops back on his chair, shuddering"—this climax having converted him to death physically and intellectually.

As the curtain falls on the singing, jeering, laughing crowd, Hugo's erotic lines emerge from the hubbub. The suggestion of hot days in the cool of the willow shade brings derisive hoots. Laughing at an iceman joke may not be real living, but it fends off the death which comes from serious love. At the end the men have stopped their rhythmic, pagan chanting, and each sings a song which suits himself. It may not lead to anything but the grave, but it is more fun and more prolonged than the love-death. Enactment of the love-death upon the stage requires the consummate skill which Eugene O'Neill possesses. Carefully building up the tension through four long, rhythmical acts, with the culmination in perhaps the lengthiest speech in any important drama, he has Parritt, Larry, and Hickey experience physical sex-death, of which the other characters recognize the virulence. But although they are forced to engage in the process through Hickey's persuasive powers during much of the play, they save themselves from succumbing at the end. And so, as O'Neill wishes, a strange friendship prevails. Brooks Atkinson notes that O'Neill's best plays "move across the stage as methodically and resolutely as a heavy battle attack and over-run strategic points with a kind of lumbering precision."[10] And so *The Iceman* does.

The most renowned director of the play, José Quintero, agrees that the structure is artistic and skillful. Of the Circle in the Square production, he says that he felt like an orchestra conductor, aware of changing tempos and themes "repeating themselves with slight variations as melodies do in a symphony."[11] He learned for the first time, he says, "the meaning of precision in drama." The play might be likened to a parody of Beethoven's Ninth with its "Hymn to Joy" at the end. The concluding words to Joy—"All mankind are brothers plighted/ Where thy gentle wings abide"—is the sentiment of the bums of Hope's bar. With Hickey

10. *New York Times*, Oct. 10, 1946.
11. "Postscript to a Journey," *Theatre Arts*, XLI (April, 1957), 28.

gone, friendship blossoms. The music critic, Charles O'Connell, wonders of Beethoven whether "such frenetic, such almost insane jubilation, on so abstract a concept"[12] can be sincerely meant, but there seems no doubt that since O'Neill himself said his play was about the working of strange friendship, he was sincere in his concrete portrayal of it. Modern symphonies, containing cacophony and disharmony, atonality and rhythmic alterations, changes of key and tempo, and mixtures of pagan rhythms with sentimental tunes, might seem more similar to O'Neill's play, which also defies traditional dramaturgical analysis. But "frenetic" is an appropriate description for the "hilariously happy" singers of thirteen different songs, varying from "She's the Sunshine of Paradise Alley" and "The Curse of an Aching Heart" to "Everybody's Doing It" by the prostitutes and the French Revolutionary "Carmagnole" extolling the sound of the cannons by Hugo.

The most thematic of the thirteen is Willie Oban's ballad, requiring three raps upon the table in place of the appropriate vulgar words concerning the actions of the sailor with the wanton maid upstairs in the tavern. Snatches of it are sung at four different times, the first as the crowd nervously waits for Hickey, and again as Oban cannot control his nervousness and sings up to the point of "I'll show you the prettiest (Rap, rap, rap on table)/ That ever you did see," before he is shushed again by the anxious alcoholics. Near the end of the gloomy birthday party, however, when the crowd taunts Hickey with having lost his wife to the iceman, and Willie substitutes, "Come up, my iceman lad," for "sailor lad" in the song, all gleefully join in, rapping with knuckles or glasses on the table for the rap, rap, rap of the chorus. Although it is not yet known that the iceman who took Evelyn is death, Hickey reveals the truth in his next speech. The erotic connotations of the song are obvious, but O'Neill, by putting the word "iceman" in place of "sailor," makes just as obvious the connection he intends between sexual love and death. It is fitting that Willie should be singing the song again and rapping rhythmically as the final curtain falls, while all partake of the booze which has made them "oreyeyed" and will shortly make them "paralyzed." Thus they may synthetically partake of the little death which is the aftermath of sexual love, and shortly of the alcoholic's death which is permanent. Whatever kind of friendship there

12. *The Victor Book of the Symphony* (New York, 1935), p. 89.

might be between men who share the dirty joke, there is nothing procreative, and the love which is procreative is merely the rap, rap, rap of the phallus, resulting in oblivion.

Besides Willie's song, the most important thematic repetition is by the old Anarchist Hugo, whose variations on "Tis cool beneath thy willow trees!" run through the play and are its curtain line. These lines are of course as erotically suggestive to the men as an iceman joke, and the satire is even greater because instead of being a coarse joke, it seems to come from some romantic poem like the *Rubáiyát* or the *Song of Songs,* or perhaps one thinks of Yeats' "Down by the Salley Gardens," but obviously the men look at it as the same old smut. The preceding line, "The days grow hot, O Babylon," is of course just as suggestive of sexual lasciviousness in that city of corruption, and perhaps the cool of the willow trees may suggest that when hot lust is satisfied, the coolness of death sets in. On five different occasions Hugo recites some variety of the lines, in one case at the end of the possibly symbolic Last Supper, with a strange mixture of Christian and pagan connotations. Hugo rejoices that "Ve vill eat birthday cake and trink champagne beneath the villow tree!" until he tastes the excellent wine which Hickey has provided, and then he complains with disgust that it is not fit to drink. Hickey accuses him of being at heart not a lover of the proletariat but a high-toned swell, who if he had the chance would drink "our blood beneath those willow trees." The imagery is of the communion, which is too a love-death in that the communicant drinks the blood of Christ who is love. But with the cynicism evident in the whole play, the intimation is that Hugo would metaphorically consume those whom he pretends to love. As to the sexual symbolism, one is reminded of Donne's "The Flea," in which love and death (of the flea who has drunk the lovers' blood) are lightly mixed.

The interwoven themes of Willie's rap, rap, rap and Hugo's hot days in Babylon emphasize the rhythm of the play as an erotic experience, through which the characters pass toward death. If it is true, as T. S. Eliot sees it, that the modern playwright understands the basis of drama to be a "form or rhythm imposed upon the world of action,"[13] *The Iceman* may profitably be examined in connection with a Hitlerian film of 1934, *Triumph des Willens.*

13. Fergusson, *Idea of a Theater,* p. 144.

Showing the strong influence of Wagner, with the music from *Tristan* in the background, it is a movie which imposes form and rhythm upon the pre-war Germanic world of der Führer. As Francis Fergusson describes this film, it shows "the yearning of the Führer and the Volk for each other, of their orgasmic junction, and of their unification in and with the one mystic German Wille."[14] After explaining how passion is aroused through nostalgic pictures of rural Germany and then built up through the sight of speeding planes and marching soldiers and finally intensified by crowds enthralled in the chant of Hitler's name, Fergusson agrees that this ritualistic love story of Hitler and Germany is "not quite a Liebestodt," but he insists that "it points to the real death which so many in the field, and in the rest of the world, were to find before the end of the march."[15] The film is not one orgasmic encounter but several little deaths, each climaxing in the desperate excitement of a gigantic crowd scene, which reminds one, says Fergusson, "of Tristan and Isolde in ecstasy affirming their mystic identity with the world." O'Neill was distraught by the rise of Nazism and the prospect of World War II. "I have been absolutely sunk by this damned debacle,"[16] he wrote Lawrence Langner in 1940. It is not surprising that he was moved in 1939 to create *The Iceman Cometh*, which, with such pertinency, imposed upon the Hell Hole world of action he had known the form and rhythm of the love-death which he saw impelling mankind to destruction.

The object of the action of *The Iceman*—men drinking themselves to the peace of death—is one O'Neill lived through at Jimmy the Priest's and the Hell Hole more than a quarter of a century before. The form and rhythm he imposed upon his world of action perfectly control it. The repetition of actions, of snatches of song, of language, of laughter at the iceman jokes, of exposition, of definition, of theorizing, of argument, of bickering, of epithet, is intrinsic. Whether love is through strange friendship or heterosexual, it moves with repetitious rhythm. The beating of soldiers' feet or the booming of guns or the chanting of crowds builds up the orgasmic nature of the love affair between the German people and Hitler, who had enough characteristics of the hermaphrodite to be the lover of all Germany, and who married his

14. *Ibid.*, p. 92.
15. *Ibid.*, p. 93.
16. Langner, *Magic Curtain*, p. 398.

47

love just before their suicides. In O'Neill's play the heterosexual love affairs which take place offstage are less real than the suggested homosexuality on stage, but for the rhythm which leads to the love-death there is no difference. The two themes of the play—that man needs illusions to survive and that love is really hate—are thus united in the rhythm of love, illustrating man's greatest illusion: that love does not lead to death.

During the twenties O'Neill had experimented with ritual in *The Fountain* and *Lazarus Laughed,* and although neither was successful in itself, each probably provided dramaturgical experience which was invaluable to him in the structure of *The Iceman Cometh.* At the time *The Ancient Mariner* was produced, O'Neill had been working on a dramatization of the fable of Ponce de León and the fountain of youth. Juan Ponce de León's search for youth in order to win a girl's love might seem a very different theme from that of *The Iceman,* but in spite of the fact that love is seen as related to God, the spiritual bridegroom, there is recognition that earthly love burns up in flaming death. The ecstasy which dissolves self in the experience of the "soaring flame of the spirit transfiguring Death" is nevertheless one aroused by Juan's vision of his beloved dying in flames. Freud has pointed out that there is "no doubt about the originally phallic view taken of tongues of flame as they shoot upwards."[17] That mystical union with God can be conceived only in terms of physical love is the theme of the song which is repeated many times: "Love is a flower . . ./ One with God but/ Ever returning/ to kiss the earth that the flower may live." So Juan must give his Beatriz to his nephew, as Death appears to him in the guise of a young girl; for life can be restored only through a new generation, which then dies. More Dionysian than Christian, the theme of love and death is that even a mystical vision of life eternal is no good without its verification in fact through a pair of young lovers. Therefore, if erotic love is necessary for the conception of holy love, but erotic love means death, there is nowhere to turn—except as in *The Iceman* to dreams, drunkenness, or, in Larry's case, to annihilating death-in-life.

In *Lazarus Laughed,* a ritualistic play stridently resounding with the ambiguities of love and death, O'Neill compounded confusion by two major incongruities. In the first place the raising of

17. *Civilization and Its Discontents,* p. 37n.

Lazarus symbolizes the miraculous power of Jesus to resurrect the dead, and is, according to the Gospel of John, presumably the reason that Jesus was so admired as he rode into Jerusalem on Palm Sunday. A writer wishing to emphasize the spirit of Christianity could not do better than to choose Lazarus as his symbol. Since O'Neill does the opposite, he is in the strange position of making this very Lazarus deny his resurrectionist and become the worshipped himself. With his virulent laughter and pagan exultation in life, he frightens the followers of Jesus. His own father curses the day his son was raised from the grave. He thinks a mocking devil dwells in Lazarus and that his daughters, Martha and Mary, thus worship the Prince of Devils. There is no harmony between Jesus' teaching, "He that hateth his life in this world shall keep it unto life eternal," and Lazarus' song, "There is only life! There is only laughter!" Contention among the tradition-oriented Jewish priests and their congregations results in death for Lazarus' father, mother, and sisters, and in deep sorrow and finally death for his wife. And Jesus is crucified—to all of which Lazarus cries his Nietzschean Yes! In contrasting the Zarathustrian and Christian attitudes toward life, O'Neill would have seemed more likely to have chosen any other figure than Lazarus to illustrate the former, because Lazarus is not a symbol of the recurring life processes of Nature.

But O'Neill, in trying to fit mythical ideas into dramatic form, is further ambiguous in making of Lazarus a Dionysus, generally conceived as the goat-god, inspirer through drink of rhapsodic song and orgiastic promiscuity, and climactically of cannibalistic consumption by the Bacchae. O'Neill had .to take great pains to make clear, therefore, that Lazarus is different from the chorus clad in goat skins, "their tanned bodies and masks daubed and stained with wine lees, in imitation of the old followers of Dionysus." Lazarus is, according to the playwright, "a positive masculine Dionysus, closest to the soil of the Grecian Gods. . . . Not the coarse, drunken Dionysus, nor the effeminate God." He represents "the wine of life stirring forever in the sap and blood and loam of things."

Imposing the name and some of the story of the Biblical Lazarus on the Greek God Dionysus and then making Lazarus an Earth deity distorts this unwieldy drama. And a further incongruity is that, although in the stage directions O'Neill insists on Lazarus'

God-like masculinity, in the action Lazarus is cold to his affectionate wife, Miriam, and even colder to the passionate Pompeia,
whose brow he lightly brushes with a kiss. Recognizing his essential
lack of warmth, she turns pitying eyes on his wife and says,
"Poor woman! How he must have tortured you," while, as the
woman scorned, she angrily charges Lazarus, "You who are neither
a man nor a god but a dead thing without desire!" Her laughter
at him is harsh and grating—the kind which O'Neill felt toward
life and which emerges from time to time in this drama in contrast
to the joyous laughter which is its theme.

Again in this scene O'Neill is caught in the dilemma of having
Lazarus represent Agape rather than Venus, to whom Dionysus is
much closer. Lazarus says of the dead Miriam, "I feel Eternal
Life made nobler by your selflessness! Love has grown purer!"
The implication here, as in *The Iceman*, is that men like their
women better dead, for the result of sexual love is their own
death. Lazarus might well be Harry Hope bemoaning the death of
his beloved Bessie. The point is further emphasized in the later
scene when, as Lazarus is being burnt alive at the stake, Pompeia
passionately throws herself into the flames and perishes with him,
while Caligula seizes a spear and runs it through the dying man,
crying with ecstasy, "I have killed God! I am death!" Of course
the ending of the play is violently erotic and hence more Dionysian than the laughter throughout. As Derek Monsey points out
in "Death in the Theatre," one of the factors which makes murder
good theater is "the sexual stimulus of sudden, particularly of
violent death."[18] And the running through of a man by a spear—a
phallic symbol unsheathed from his body—is representative of the
homosexual love of the barracks. As hard as O'Neill tried to modify
Dionysus, he did not succeed; the play carried him away, and at
the end his hero is the old Dionysus of violent love and death,
troublesomely named Lazarus.

Besides Nietzsche, O'Neill was influenced by the theater of Max
Reinhardt, which combined the religiousness of the Oberammer-
gau Passion Play with the spirit of pagan music, song, and dance.
Therefore in *Lazarus Laughed*, O'Neill tried to carry out the idea
of saying yes to life—to all of its pain and joy—and he showed
an understanding of the kind of pagan ritual which Nietzsche
described in *The Birth of Tragedy* as originating in the Bacchic

18. *Theatre Arts*, XLVI, 4 (April, 1962), 20.

chorus of the Greeks and continuing even to the Middle Ages, wherein "dancers of St. John and St. Vitus . . . were whirled from place to place under this same Dionysian impulse."[19] Even the Chorus of Old Men in the play, who try to avoid being carried away by the ecstasy of Lazarus and his followers, succumb. An aged Orthodox Jew "fights the spell but cannot control his jerking body," and the old men "begin to feel impelled by the rhythm and laughter, their feet move, their bodies sway." And finally both the followers of Jesus and the Orthodox are swept away by the reveling followers of Lazarus. "They begin to weave in and out, clasping each other's hands now and then, moving mechanically in jerky steps." O'Neill describes their movement as "peculiar" perhaps in order to allow actors to use their imagination or to avoid a more explicitly sexual word. As they become more intoxicated by the movement the dancers turn animal-like, raising their hands like threatening talons, as they reach out to Lazarus as a sacrificial victim, all the time hopping, milling, and twisting in a parody of the dance of the followers of Lazarus. Either—sardonic parody or authentic ritual—is a dance of death, for Crassus says of the true followers: "They charged upon us laughing! They tore our swords away from us, laughing, and we laughed with them. They stabbed themselves dancing as though it were a festival. They died laughing in one another's arms."

O'Neill has expressed explicitly in this play the joy of dying felt by men, whether it be in orgiastic reveling or as the bride of Christ. In a less subtle way he has put what A. E. Housman so admirably expresses about the sexual pleasure of dying in "I Did Not Lose My Heart in Summer's Even":

> I did not lose my heart in summer's even,
> When roses to the moonrise burst apart:
> When plumes were under heel and lead was flying,
> In blood and smoke and flame I lost my heart.
>
> I lost it to a soldier and a foeman,
> A chap that did not kill me, but he tried,
> That took the saber straight and took it striking
> And laughed and kissed his hand to me and died.

Shakespeare, who knows all, knows that the soldier prefers death on the battlefield to death in bed, for his sexual pleasure there is

19. Trans. Francis Golffing (New York, 1956), p. 22.

greater. When Coriolanus, driven from his native Rome, approaches Aufidius, his former enemy, he is received ecstatically by this soldier with whom he has formerly grappled.

> Why thou Mars!
> . . . Thou hast beat me out
> Twelve several times, and I have nightly since
> Dreamt of encounters 'twixt thyself and me;
> We have been down together in my sleep,
> Unbuckling helms, fisting each other's throat,
> And wak'd half dead with nothing. (IV.v.)

As if this were not enough, Aufidius further claims:

> Know thou first,
> I lov'd the maid I married; never man
> Sigh'd truer breath; but that I see thee here,
> Thou noble thing! more dances my rapt heart
> Than when I first my wedded mistress saw
> Bestride my threshhold. (IV.v.)

Shakespeare shows the erotic attraction of war—of killing and being killed. The great sensuous paintings of the Renaissance of a lightly clad Venus beside a dark-armored Mars who lays his hand upon her bare thigh or shoulder expressed more openly than we like to admit today that killing and being killed are sexual pleasures—Venus and Mars in one. O'Neill, having experimented with rhythmic pantomimic chorus scenes in *Lazarus Laughed*, transferred covertly, perhaps partly unknown to himself, such scenes to *The Iceman*. Brooks Atkinson noted the ritualistic basis of the play: "The Lord knows they [the characters of *The Iceman*] talk too much . . . but it is good talk—racy, angry, comic drumbeats on the lid of doom, and a strong undercurrent of elemental drama washes the gloomy charnel-house where they sit waiting."[20] An echo from the earlier play also carries over in Larry's remark that his function in life is "observing the cannibals do their death dance." The dreaming and drinking, the healing and hurting, the loving and hating, the singing and sorrowing, the going out and coming back in Hope's bar are so realistically worked into the action of the play that they are not recognizable as orgiastic choric movements, but the emotional effect of them is telling.

20. *New York Times*, Oct. 10, 1946.

In *Lazarus Laughed,* a seemingly most inappropriate place for it, O'Neill also revealed his relish for a dirty joke—not of the iceman variety, but of a seventeenth-century-conceit variety that love is death in bed. Caligula is advised that the only way to get rid of Lazarus is to kill him.

> *Caligula:* But if he knows a charm against death how
> could he be slain, old fool?
> *Crassus:* (gruffly) Bah! (Then with grim humor) Death
> in bed I suspect.

Perhaps O'Neill knew Dryden's play, *Marriage-à-la-Mode,* containing the song in which Caelia, locked in ardent embrace with Alexis, appeals to him, for her sake, to die more slowly.

> The youth, though in haste,
> And breathing his last,
> In pity dy'd slowly, while she dy'd more fast:
> Till at length she cry'd, Now my dear, now let us go,
> Now die, my *Alexis,* and I will die too. (IV.iii.)

The iceman is "breathin' hard" and "coming" as fast as possible in O'Neill's later play, but the foundation is laid in *Lazarus Laughed,* where the whole question of life and death is set against the rhythmic, masked-crowd ritual which led in ancient times to the great Greek drama, and in ours fortunately, through those Dionysian elements which O'Neill could not keep out of it, to *The Iceman Cometh.* Leonard Chabrowe expresses the opinion in "Dionysus in *The Iceman Cometh*" that had it not been for the dramatic experience he gained from *Lazarus Laughed,* O'Neill could not have conceived of *The Iceman.* O'Neill's theory that "only through ritual could the audience be made to experience a Dionysian communion with life itself"[21] carried over into the later play.

Besides a resemblance of the chorus of men in Hope's bar to the choruses of the earlier play, Chabrowe notes a correspondence between Hickey, Parritt, and Larry and the leading characters of Lazarus, Tiberius, and Caligula. Hickey, of course, like Lazarus, is reborn to a new peace by his killing of Evelyn, and also comes to bring happiness to the men. And the loving, but neglected wives of both are brought to their death by their husbands. Parritt, like Tiberius, hates his domineering mother. And Larry, like

21. *Modern Drama,* IV, 4 (Feb., 1962), 377-88.

Caligula, is death-oriented. But more important than similarity of plot or character is the difference in the language and tone of the two plays. The imagery of Lazarus is monumental and pretentious, as when Caligula, converted by Lazarus, shouts, "No lust for death. My corpse no longer rots in my heart!" before declaring that if all Rome does not accede to his laughter, he will cut off their heads. In comparison, Larry's simple curse, "Be God, I'm the only real convert to death Hickey made here," rings with authenticity. And most important is the fact that the blatant ritual in *Lazarus* O'Neill toned down in *The Iceman* and further concealed through degenerate characters speaking illiterate slang in a naturalistic setting. Then with a thick layer of drunken bawdry over the essentially orgiastic nature of its love-as-death theme, he buried it. The ritualistic nature of the play is therefore felt and not overtly perceived.

In an effort at enlightenment, critics have therefore examined the play in both emotional and rational terms. In either they have found a unity and unalterable plan which some directors and actors who have been involved in producing it have not appreciated.[22] This is not to say, however, that the play when read has an organization which when staged it does not. Analyzed in detail, or in the large units of acts, or in the use of language, or in its characters, setting, and action, it has both theoretically and practically a consistent aim which the playwright perseveres in proving and illustrating, and which Quintero's successful staging verified. Approached emotionally, the whole movement of the play may be seen, as Eugene M. Waith does, as "the advance and retreat of a huge wave."[23] In view of the many references to the bar as submerged in the bottom of the sea, and to the reform wave which Hickey sets going and in which the men almost drown, the first act may be seen as the passive stage where the turbulence below does not appear on the surface of the water. As the men are aroused to action, the wave appears to be beaten in fury, and at the end it subsides as the men go back to their dreaming and drinking. Within this structure are many small waves, in which the characters are helplessly washed back and forth in

22. See Eric Bentley, "Trying to Like O'Neill," *In Search of Theater* (New York, 1953), pp. 233-47.
23. "Eugene O'Neill: An Exercise in Unmasking," *Educational Theatre Journal*, XIII (1961), 189.

currents before they are carried over the crest to crash and subside once more into quiet.

Again O'Neill might seem to be parodying *Tristan and Isolde,* for Isolde sings, "In the sea of pleasure's/ Billowing roll,/ In the ether waves/ Knelling and toll,/ In the world-breath's/ Wavering whole—/ To drown in, go down in—/ Lost in swoon—greatest boon!" This height of romantic ecstasy in the love-death O'Neill makes into the "coming" of the iceman, for as Doris Falk points out, O'Neill may cloak his meaning but "the Silenus wears the phallus and desecrates shrines with jocular vulgarity."[24] Another conception of death by drowning that is in contrast to O'Neill's is Whitman's in his great ode to death, "When Lilacs Last in the Dooryard Bloom'd." To the poet, "lovely and soothing death" is a "dark mother," of whom he says that he longs to be "lost in the loving floating ocean of thee,/ Laved in the flood of thy bliss O Death." To Whitman death is the great womb to which mortals return, nestling in infantile comfort against the encompassing body of the "strong deliveress." "Over the tree-tops I float thee a song," he exults. All the images of water in this section of this hymn to death express the gentleness of the mother toward the child: they are of undulating waves, calmly rolling ocean, cleansing swells, rising and sinking waves. None are images of violence, as in *The Iceman* where the eddies that propel the men forward and out are severe and shocking. The turbulence of sexual encounter is contrary to Whitman's mood but essential to O'Neill's, who desecrates the shrine of romantic love and also that of spiritual rebirth from a mystical mother, for death is not a loving bridegroom or a gentle deliveress.

But with the cynical attitude of the creators of the powerful movie *Dr. Strangelove,* O'Neill would have been in sympathy. In this masterpiece of obscene pessimism, King Kong, the burly Texas pilot of the plane that destroys mankind, straddles the bomb named Lolita and soars down to perish in an orgasm which even the Titans who made this world might envy. In spite of his success with women, and his talk of how potent his Daddy still is, and of how he likes his women "prime cut and double grade A premium," he still feels "incomplete" without combat. Only in the kind of magnificent *Liebestod* he undergoes can he find completeness—a completeness which also completes mankind.

24. "That Paradox, O'Neill," *Modern Drama,* VI, 3 (Dec., 1963), 223.

In his metaphor of sexual love as the consumption of a juicy steak, he reveals the connection he feels between love and death. But only in the three ecstatic minutes of the ride upon Lolita between heaven and earth, before the twenty-megaton explosion, does he reach true fulfillment—love and death in one. We are all urged in this parable of "strange love" to "Love the Bomb," and shown the example in Major Kong of one who thoroughly does. The crazed laughter with which the audience greets the end of the world would have delighted O'Neill, who in *The Great God Brown* has Dion Anthony build a cathedral where the people "worship the ironic Silenus who tells them the best good is never to have been born," and who in *The Iceman* shows that love means death.

From the point of view of the play as an intellectual creation, *The Iceman* also has obvious unity of action. According to Norman Chaitin, "regardless of whether we can agree on the real meaning of it, *Iceman* is the most powerful theorem any playwright has ever put on paper."[25] It might seem strange that the meaning of a powerful theorem should be arguable, but it is true that O'Neill often did not reveal his intentions and in fact enjoyed making his audiences puzzled. Doris Falk explains: "While O'Neill often railed at critics for not understanding him, he just as often played a game designed to lead them away from the truth."[26] Consequently, even though by repeated examples—some think to the extent of boredom—he proved his case, it is possible that he intentionally beclouded the point. Chaitin contends that O'Neill is a thinker rather than an intuitive playwright. Contrary as this view is to that of many others, it may be true, but whether an intuitive playwright or not, O'Neill was intuitively right about human nature. He knew that "the blood of the martyrs is the seed of the church." That blood and semen are one in the human psyche was as clear to him as that the perfect completion of the love relationship of those who have drunk of the nectar is, like that of Tristan and Isolde, death. And so the theorem, reinforced by intuition and proved by logic, which is contained in the title and to which can be put *Q.E.D.* at the end is: Love is death.

To Mary McCarthy also *The Iceman* "has the structure of an argument," but she also implies a rhythm which is nonintellectual

25. "Power of Daring," p. 240.
26. "That Paradox, O'Neill," p. 222.

when she points out that "the characters roar over and over again" when one of them asks, "How is your wife getting along with the iceman?" As to the play's metaphor, she is even more critical: "And though death is the iceman, the joke is not appreciably refined by this symbolic treatment; rather it is death that is coarsened."[27] Thinking to be derogatory, she has nevertheless caught the spirit of what O'Neill intends. He does not wish to sanctify death, but to make it synonymous with lustful passion which destroys life. She complains that O'Neill is the only man in the world who is still laughing at the iceman joke or pondering its implications, without realizing that the joke is worth pondering as O'Neill does it. Her final condemnation of the play—"Its solitariness inside its rigid structure suggests the prison or the asylum or the sound of a man laughing in a square empty room"—is one that O'Neill would probably have considered high praise. If she had said *tomb* instead of *room,* and *jeering* instead of *laughing,* she would have expressed his intention even more accurately, because room implies too much of life and laughter too much of pagan joy. Although there is much humor in the play, O'Neill's handling of the setting, the characters, and the action gives it all a sardonic twinge.

It is true, however, that the structure is rigid—partly because it is an argument, inductive by virtue of one case after another produced in evidence of the general conclusion, and partly because it is a ritual, pagan in rhythm, like the wild dithyrambic rites for Dionysus which led to the god's love-death and consumption by the delirious Bacchantes. Its genius, then, lies in the structure of the action, which so well portrays the theme of the title, and is both rational and emotional.

27. "Eugene O'Neill—Dry Ice," in *Sights and Spectacles* (New York, 1956), p. 85.

CONCLUSION

If O'Neill perhaps learned more of how to handle pagan ritual from *Lazarus Laughed* than from his other plays, the ones concerning marriage, like *Servitude, Welded,* and *All God's Chillun Got Wings,* helped him formulate the love which kills in *The Iceman.* In *Welded,* which deals with a couple hopelessly linked together by bonds of passion, O'Neill shrilly exposes Cape, who wishes to kill his wife because he loves her so much that he cannot live without her. After debating whether it would not be better to kill himself, he concludes that this solution is hopeless as well: "I can't. Our love must live on in me. There's no death for it." Sensing that his love is death, he mutters incoherently, "You're the perfect death." And in a later play, *Dynamo,* love results in violent death, as Reuben, after succumbing to sexual love with Ada beneath the huge dynamo, shoots her through the breast and then dies by seizing the carbon brushes of the dynamo. He is electrocuted with "a moan that is a mingling of pain and loving consummation." His affair with the dynamo is slightly incestuous, since this moan dies into a sound "that is like the crooning of a baby," and Reuben cries, "Mother! Never let me go from you again." This gross love-death excludes the dramatic empathy which O'Neill engendered by more subtlety for the characters in *The Iceman*—Hickey, Hope, Parritt, Jimmy Tomorrow, and perhaps Larry—who have been smothered in a love-hate relationship with a woman.

When he came to write *Days Without End,* O'Neill tried to combine marital and Christian love, but without great success. The hero wishes to kill a love which is overwhelming, and the devout priest, quoting from "The Hound of Heaven," tries to persuade him of the futility of evading God's love. At the end the devilish part of John Loving lies dead at the foot of the Cross while the revitalized and holy part stands ecstatically in the shape of a Cross, exclaiming, "Love lives forever! Death is dead!" But only vestigial Christian symbolism remains in *The Iceman,* except for the title. As Cyrus Day points out, Hope's birthday party is reminiscent of the Last Supper with Hickey supplying the wine, as well as a derisive portrait of the Savior whose aim is to bring peace,

58

but who proves to be as lost as his victims.[1] Parritt as Judas, who betrays and then kills himself, and the prostitutes as the three Marys fulfill no special function, but Hickey's gift of gab, which he got from a father "who could sell those Hoosier hayseeds building lots along the Golden Street!" does, in keeping with the tone of the play, satirize Christian sermonizing.

As time tempered O'Neill's enthusiasm for the literal use of pagan ritual, so it did for the obviously Christian, but the question of the love relationship in human beings haunted him from first to last. Thus in *Mourning Becomes Electra*, no matter what other motivation the characters may be impelled by, it is true, as H. Steinhauer notes, that "the series of catastrophes which stalk the House of Mannon are caused by repeated attempts to thwart the natural expression of the sex instinct."[2] Doris Falk concludes that "the entire story turns on the sexual inadequacies of the Mannon men."[3] Their inadequacy as living men is further emphasized by the death mask which they and their mansion wear. To Orin, his dead father appears more natural than when alive. And Dr. Blake, surmising that the first night home with a beautiful wife was too much for Mannon's weak heart, opines that "It was love killed Ezra," to which a neighbor replies with a salacious chuckle, "I can imagine worse ways of dying." The serious tone of this mammoth tragedy of ten years earlier did not prevent O'Neill's inserting the kind of *double entendre* on the love-death on which he based *The Iceman*. In plays like *The Great God Brown, Desire Under the Elms,* and *A Moon for the Misbegotten,* the sexual man-woman theme is related to the mother-son theme. But it matters not what the relationship is, the devouring Mother-Earth, who is a whore in *The Great God Brown,* will comfort but consume man in the end. Between Abby and Eben in *Desire Under the Elms* love flowers, and in spite of the sordid situation, rises to spiritual heights, but its result too is death, to which the lovers go with a subconscious recognition that on this earth passion, one way or another, leads to the same inevitable end. In *Moon for the Misbegotten*, sexual love with a whore for revenge upon the mother who left him to life while she

1. "The Iceman and the Bridegroom," *Modern Drama*, I, 1 (May, 1958), 3-9.
2. "Eros and Psyche: A Nietzschean Motif in Anglo-American Literature," *Modern Language Notes*, LXIV (April, 1949), 228.
3. "That Paradox, O'Neill," pp. 225-26.

enjoyed the peace of death, has been the death of Jim Tyrone. Like a pietà, in what Eric Bentley calls O'Neill's monument,[4] Josie sits all night cradling the dipsomaniac as she grieves for "the dead hugged to my breast."

In *Strange Interlude*, Nina, who from the woman's point of view wishes God were female, sees the father himself as death: "Death . . . my father . . . comes between me and happiness." With ambiguity piled on ambiguity, O'Neill sees woman as the seducer, and yet here it is the man who brings about her death. Of course, through smothering love, she frequently brings about his. Dryden's short poem about Alexis and Caelia concludes:

> Thus entranced they did lie,
> Till Alexis did try
> To recover new breath, that again he might die;
> Then often they died; but the more they did so,
> The nymph died more quick, and the shepherd more slow.

It is necessary for the iceman to take over when the husband is compelled to leave off. The drunks in Hope's bar have a common bond of unsuccess in the economic and social realms, but their strange friendship is engendered perhaps even more by their recognition of a common inadequacy in the sexual.

Although *The Iceman* is said to show influences of other plays, such as Gorki's *The Lower Depths* and Ibsen's *The Wild Duck*, the essence of it is O'Neill's own. Gorki's dark cellar, with its congregation of dreaming wrecks who are visited by the compassionate pilgrim Luka, does bear some resemblance to *The Iceman*, but although passionate love does result in murder, the play's theme is not that love is death but that man is unique and that life's processes are bearable if tempered by illusion and love. Also Luka brings love with him, whereas Hickey brings death. In *The Wild Duck* Gregers rips the veil of pretense from a happy household, bringing not happiness, but misery to all and death to a young girl. Gregers' subconscious motives have been destructive like those of Hickey, who admits at one point that he wants to destroy the happiness of the men rather than to bring them peace. But except for the fact that all three plays illustrate that illusion is better than truth, they are dissimilar. The tone of

4. "Eugene O'Neill's Pietà," in *The Dramatic Event* (Boston, 1954), p. 30.

the continental plays is not sardonic but pitying, and even somewhat hopeful because of the creative love which does sometimes exist, whereas to O'Neill love is always destructive or else exists only beyond a romantic horizon.

In *The Iceman Cometh*, O'Neill illustrates through his unique dramaturgy that love is man's undoing. His characters act out their parts against a background of physical, social, and psychological hell. There is no holy Beatrice to bring about their redemption. Woman to them is contaminated and contagious with the virulent disease of death. Even Dante's vision of female savior could not be of a woman with whom he had known earthly love, but only one worshipped from afar. In his recent play, *Tiny Alice*, Edward Albee combines profane and holy love-death upon the stage when the lay priest Julian, surrounded by the flowing robes of Miss Alice and pressed against her hot body, envisions himself as a Christian martyr devoured by a lion and feels "the lion's belly pressed on my chest." He murmurs, "There is a wound in me, the warm dark flow . . . runs down my belly . . . to . . . bathing my groin," and then continues incoherently, "the chest fanged and the soft hard tongue and the *blood* . . . ENTERS."[5] Blood and semen become indistinguishable to Julian. Albee intimates the same mother love for woman (Miss Alice may represent the Virgin Mary) which O'Neill finds inseparable from sexual love. Albee also involves the Christian parable of holy love with the sexual, for only the virginal can remain immortal. The iceman can "fill your box," according to the old barroom song, but he is really profane death.

So O'Neill, like Albee, has combined from out of his subconscious various images of love as death. His characters come to the slow revelation of themselves through Hickey's proddings. Parritt gradually appreciates that whore and mother are the same, and Hickey's moment of self-revelation shows him that wife and bitch are one. Larry has long since seen that love means "de killin'." Chuck concludes about wives: "De minute your back is turned, dey're cheatin' wid de iceman or someone." And all come to sense that Eve, the temptress, brings mortality to man. In a bottom-of-the-sea charnel house, against a background of social disruption, the characters plunge toward the life of reality in a series of seismic waves, which carry them to the brink of death.

5. New York, 1965, II.iii.

But at the end they are drifting about in waters, which, if stagnant, are at least not dashing into the maelstrom of sexual death. And so their swan song is a discordant but jubilant hymn to brotherly love as the alcoholic content of their blood rises toward the fatal level. John Gassner believes that *The Iceman* "is perhaps the most relentlessly depressing drama written by any modern playwright."[6] And Wolcott Gibbs wrote that the play was "so emotionally disturbing and intellectually demanding" that he did not appreciate it in 1946. But at the Circle in the Square production he was "prepared for the conception of absolute despair" and found the play a tragedy that "states a terrible truth with extraordinary power and compassion."[7] O'Neill has put the essence of the play in the mouth of the cynical hero of *More Stately Mansions,* written during the same period: ". . . the obvious fact is that their lives [men's] are without any meaning whatever—that human life is a silly disappointment, a liar's promise, a perpetual in-bankruptcy for debts we never contracted, a daily appointment with peace and happiness in which we wait day after day, hoping against hope, and when the bride or the bridegroom cometh, we discover we are kissing death."[8] Albee's hero meets such a fate. A sacrificial victim, dressed in white from tie to shoes, Julian is deserted by his bride, Miss Alice, on his wedding day, but before she leaves her dying bridegroom, she presents him with a ghostly mask to kiss.

Mary McCarthy rightly points out, however, that *The Iceman* is like no other play ever written, "estranged from all influences and impressions."[9] In spite of superficial resemblances to others, it is unique. It is O'Neill's creation out of his own life (with its haunted family in early years and its unhappy marriages later)

6. *A Treasury of the Theatre* (3rd College Edition; New York, 1960), p. 788.

7. *New Yorker,* XXXII, 14 (May 26, 1956), 72-74.

8. Donald Gallup, ed. of script revised by Karl Ragnar Gierow (New Haven: Yale University Press, 1964), p. 179. Also, it should not be overlooked by those critics who see more humor than gloom in *The Iceman* that, according to the Gelbs (p. 855), O'Neill felt the pessimism of it to be so deep that the postwar audience would not be able to accept the play until after disillusionment with the peace had set in. Hemingway, at the conclusion of the war in "Second Poem to Mary" (which Hemingway orally recorded for A. E. Hotchner), expresses a like cynicism. Asking of the soldier, "Do you take this old whore death for thy lawful wedded wife?" he insists upon the thrice-repeated answer, "I do. I do. I do."

9. "Eugene O'Neill—Dry Ice," p. 85.

and his own experiments with the dramatic form. He wrote of *The Iceman*: "I have a confident hunch that this play, as drama, is one of the best things I've ever done. In some ways, perhaps *the* best."[10] Although he was not a theater-goer himself—apparently preferring the bicycle races—his judgment in this case was accurate. If he wrote the play in the midst of despair, the painting of despair saved him from self-destruction. He said of his play-writing, "You can't keep a hop head off his dope for long." As in a narcotized state, he made his private dirty joke about the iceman the essence of his play, and with the semantic blatancy of dreams he labeled the two detectives who close in on Hickey at the end, Moran (death) and Lieb (love), and made Lieb young and Moran middle-aged but gave them otherwise no individualized characteristics. He gave Hickey the slang name for a corpse, "hick"[11] (making Hickman mean dead man), and added to the play's semantic connotation by giving him the first name of Theodore (gift of God). Larry, whose last name is Slade (slayed), reiterates throughout the play that the gift of God is death. But it is Lieb who slips the handcuffs on the victim's wrists. So O'Neill had his private guffaw at the audience, who he was sure did not really understand this play which he knew in his bones was very good. Seriously he wrote, "there are moments in it that suddenly strip the secret soul of a man stark naked, not in cruelty or moral superiority, but with an understanding compassion which sees him as a victim of the ironies of life and of himself."[12] To expose life's victims in a play so structured as to illustrate by its form and rhythm, as well as by its language and content, the inevitability of death through love is a masterly accomplishment. O'Neill's own, *The Iceman*, nevertheless, speaks with psychic universality. O'Neill has skillfully imposed the rhythm of life upon the world of action which he portrays to make a play which is one in form and content, and in which the theme that love is death is the chief irony, for man nourishes and lives by the illusion that love is life.

10. Langner, p. 398.
11. Egil Tornquist, "Personal Nomenclature in the Plays of O'Neill," *Modern Drama*, VIII, 4 (Feb., 1966), 371.
12. Langner, p. 398.

UNIVERSITY OF FLORIDA MONOGRAPHS

Humanities

No. 1: *Uncollected Letters of James Gates Percival*, edited by Harry R. Warfel

No. 2: *Leigh Hunt's Autobiography: The Earliest Sketches*, edited by Stephen F. Fogle

No. 3: *Pause Patterns in Elizabethan and Jacobean Drama*, by Ants Oras

No. 4: *Rhetoric and American Poetry of the Early National Period*, by Gordon E. Bigelow

No. 5: *The Background of The Princess Casamassima*, by W. H. Tilley

No. 6: *Indian Sculpture in the John and Mable Ringling Museum of Art*, by Roy C. Craven, Jr.

No. 7: *The Cestus. A Mask*, edited by Thomas B. Stroup

No. 8: *Tamburlaine, Part I, and Its Audience*, by Frank B. Fieler

No. 9: *The Case of John Darrell: Minister and Exorcist*, by Corinne Holt Rickert

No. 10: *Reflections of the Civil War in Southern Humor*, by Wade H. Hall

No. 11: *Charles Dodgson, Semeiotician*, by Daniel F. Kirk

No. 12: *Three Middle English Religious Poems*, edited by R. H. Bowers

No. 13: *The Existentialism of Miguel de Unamuno*, by José Huertas-Jourda

No. 14: *Four Spiritual Crises in Mid-Century American Fiction*, by Robert Detweiler

No. 15: *Style and Society in German Literary Expressionism*, by Egbert Krispyn

No. 16: *The Reach of Art: A Study in the Prosody of Pope*, by Jacob H. Adler

No. 17: *Malraux, Sartre, and Aragon as Political Novelists*, by Catharinė Savage

No. 18: *Las Guerras Carlistas y el Reinado Isabelino en la Obra de Ramón del Valle-Inclán*, por María Dolores Lado

No. 19: *Diderot's Vie de Sénèque: A Swan Song Revised*, by Douglas A. Bonneville

No. 20: *Blank Verse and Chronology in Milton*, by Ants Oras

No. 21: *Milton's Elisions*, by Robert O. Evans

No. 22: *Prayer in Sixteenth-Century England*, by Faye L. Kelly

No. 23: *The Strangers: The Tragic World of Tristan L'Hermite*, by Claude K. Abraham

No. 24: *Dramatic Uses of Biblical Allusion in Marlowe and Shakespeare*, by James H. Sims

No. 25: *Doubt and Dogma in Maria Edgeworth*, by Mark D. Hawthorne

No. 26: *The Masses of Francesco Soriano*, by S. Philip Kniseley

No. 27: *Love as Death in The Iceman Cometh*, by Winifred Dusenbury Frazer

B&T 2800